M000215468

RUNNING

WITH MY EMOTIONS

Written by

Brady N. Bell

"Love is the problem.
Love is the answer."

-Brady N. Bell

Copyright © 2020 by Brady Bell

All rights reserved. No part of this book may be reproduced or used in any manner without written permission of the copyright owner except for the use of quotations in a book review.

FIRST EDITION

ISBN 978-0-578-23276-8

bradynbell.com

Table of Contents

Preface

Why can't we control ourselves? Why is it that we are so compulsive when it comes to things we know we shouldn't be doing? Is it our human nature that leads us blindly into our desires? Are we just ignorant and accept our weaknesses?

See we have an aspect within all of us that controls what we do. There's this little voice that talks to us. It wants things no matter if they are good or bad for us.

Why can't we resist what we know isn't good for us? Why do we tend to play with fire when we know we will get burned? It's as if we have a part of us that is not us but it's leading the way most of the time.

We have to regain control of ourselves and I believe the only way to do that is to get to know the real you. The "you" that you have always wanted to be. The "you" that's in control in an out of control world. I believe the only way to get to know yourself is to look deep within your emotions.

How do you respond in high stress situations or life changing events? Ask yourself that!

Our emotions control our responses but how do you control your emotions? Our emotions are not the main source of our lack of control over our lives, but they are the main manipulation point.

People and worldly objects play a big part in how our emotions are construed. How can you be truly free if you're still under the control of material objects that play on your emotions?

How do you take back control? Again, you have to find your internal self. Your true being is inside you begging to be let free.

Almost everything can be controlled once you've mastered your mindfulness. Once you're aware of your habits that you don't like, you should be able to mindfully stop doing them. Like smoking or eating too much. Once you're aware of your habits from an internal perspective, you can stop yourself from acting them out. Same can be said for your emotions and the responses they cause.

I am at fault for allowing myself to be controlled by my emotions. What you're about to read is my story. The one I've been telling myself. It's a story of reflection and self-discovery too but the choice is mine to either let it go and run with it or just keep telling myself the same shitty story. I have a choice to change and so do you. Accepting who you are now is the first step to creating a life worth living for.

This life was given to me to live and live it I shall.

Introduction:

What How Why

Chapter 1

Clear as Mud

I am an emotional train wreck. Always have been and hopefully won't always be. As a young child I could never control my emotions. I always cried. It didn't matter if I was sad, mad, disappointed or confused. I always cried over the issue. I couldn't control my emotions as a child and am still struggling to do so as an adult.

Although, as I grew older into adolescence, I learned to bury my feelings deep inside. My main reason for doing so was to reduce my social embarrassment and save as much as a good perception of myself in other's eyes as I could. I needed friends! We all need friends but more importantly, friends who like us and want to be around us.

We don't need friends who we think are our friends but are actually just being nice to us, because they feel sorry for how pitiful we look.

As a kid, I didn't like people making fun of me and putting me down because I was different. Why did I continue to hang around those people? I needed friends and any kind of human interaction I could get. I wanted to feel needed. You may be able to relate to my story, which is great, but if you can't that's okay too. Either way, I hope you get a laugh from some of the episodes of my life or at least enjoy my perception of the world that I'm about to ramble through for the next few chapters. It's different, to say the least.

I'll also note that even though this could be categorized as a motivational book, it's not your normal motivational book. Most motivational books get you to go out and do something, or change some aspect of yourself. Well, if this is a motivational book, its main purpose is to get you to stop doing stupid things that cause pain and suffering in your life. Like clinging to people who are dragging you down, or mentally beating yourself up for not meeting your expectations. At the very least it may motivate you to perceive the world differently.

As I outline my perceived mistakes in the following chapters, hopefully you can learn from them, so you don't make the same mistakes I have.

We can learn a ton from one another if we can share our most embarrassing or darkest parts of life. I'll share some of mine but justifiably, not all of them. Don't do what I've done. Learn from it.

Since the title of this book may not be clear, let's get clear on that as well. Throughout this book I'm going to try to analyze periods of my life and understand why I did the things I did through reflecting on how I felt at that point in time. A lot of what happened in my past can all be related to certain emotions or feelings that we all experience day to day. Understanding what the trigger is to that emotion, or how these emotions flow into one another, is a good way to start to grab control of your life, and to not allow yourself to be ruled by your emotional responses.

Even though I may be telling a story about my life and the events that changed my thought process, and outlook on life, this is not an autobiography. More accurately, it's an auto-discovery book. By writing down events that have occurred throughout my entire life, thus far, and going through all the data points so I can see what I have done wrong or may have been successful at, I can fully discover who I am. How can one write an autobiography if they have not discovered who they truly are?

To be even clearer, as to why I decided to put my collection of thoughts down on paper, I needed something concrete to reflect on in my older age. Something that would catalog my current perception of the world and how I feel about life itself.

Everything I've written here is not for your benefit. This book is for myself, written by me and for the reminder of who I am now, and who I once was. I'm writing this book for my own sanity. This book is important to me because I am important to me. I hope you feel lucky enough to get to read about the importance of myself.

My sanity in this psychotic world is the most important aspect to the longevity of my life. If you wish to tag along in my adventure, I'll be glad to have you by my side, but I only request that you hold yourself in the same regard.

If you happen to gain something from my words, then that's great. Good for you. Take my knowledge and go forth to conquer yourself as well.

Look, we are the weirdest things in the world, and I cannot grasp why the hell we exist. I truly do not get why we do the things we do as human beings but I believe the emotions are the root cause.

So, I'll try to convey what emotions I may have had during certain situations I've been through and what justification I have for my weirdness. I may not detail all emotions in my writings because I believe some fall under other feelings or may be explained through my interpretation of a specific event.

Also, I may not have felt the same way in certain situations that you may have felt. I may not have experienced the true meaning of the emotion. There is also the aspect that I know I have not felt the extreme conditions of any given emotion. I do not believe my writings to be meaningful to others, nor do I think my writings will heal you in some manner.

I truly just want to explain my interpretations of what I have been through so far in my life and try to relate as much as possible to those out there that may have experienced the same, or similar instances.

We all go through hardships. We don't all go through the same hardships. Each one of us has our own capacity to push through resistance. We have limits, but they are not where you think they are. They are much further out than you may believe.

Some of us have more grit than others and can go further beyond our perceived limits of our thresholds. Some of us can go harder than others if put in high stress situations, due to our fight or flight responses that we inherited from our ancestors.

The majority of us can go through more small bursts of hardships, than those who can maintain through a long rut of hell. Regardless of how much grit you have to withstand suffering, you're still suffering.

We are all different, but in a sense, we are all the same. Our similarities are our sufferings. Some of us suffer more than others. Some suffer longer. Some suffer more often. The fact still stands that we all suffer in one way or another.

Try accepting that our similarities in suffering are what should bring us together and are not to be used to differentiate between one another. Who cares how you suffer! I go through tough times too. Some are self-inflicted and some are random acts of fuckery.

Some of the other topics that I will hit on in this book have to do with me trying to figure out the meaning behind my emotions. If there is any way I can be more aware of my projected feelings into the world and also control them in such a manner, I hope that it may bring me peace, within this crazy roller coaster ride of a life, as a human being.

I want to fully understand the whys behind the feelings that certain emotions can bring about, and discover more about myself and how I've dealt with them in the past by writing them all out. This is so I can understand the reasoning behind why I've done what I've done, but also control my emotional responses moving forward so I can take back the reins of my life.

Now, I'll also give some advice on what I should have done in certain situations or what I have learned from the process of failing in those past situations but, one thing to note is, failure is valuable information to have as an individual. If we do not question our previous actions, how can we ever know if we are on the right path in life? If all we're doing is making mistakes, does that mean we're on the right path?

There is no true answer as to why we are the way we are, but maybe through writing this book I'll discover a little more about why I am the way I am, and possibly answer the question I've been diligently searching for my entire life. Who am I, really?

I have been asking myself that question more often and I hope while reading this book you will ask yourself that as well. We all need to know who we are if we want to be an authentic individual. What I mean by that is, if you're authentic, then you're being true to who you are. You are not pretending to be someone else. You are being you.

What I have determined is that once you start to do things your way, without influence, and in an authentic manner to your beliefs, you will be more aware of yourself and who you are in this world. Whether that builds your integrity or if you happen to become more of an asshole, that all depends on your morals and your perception of other human beings.

Morals play a big part into who you are or how you act. In this book, you will start to see and interpret my morals. It is the code I live by. I have to find out why I have the morals I do and digging up my past may be the only way to find the answer to when I obtained them.

What's your history? What's influenced you? What are your morals? Are you an asshole? If that's the case, then I hope you strive to be a better human being because nobody likes an asshole. More importantly no one will listen to you, respect you, or give a fuck if you die.

My own hope is not only to potentially determine the answer to some of my own questions about life and who I am, hopefully I'm not an asshole, but also figure out how to be an emotionally responsible human being in society, and not turn into an old grouchy ass hat of a man. Plus crying over everything not going the way I want in life isn't healthy as an adult. It may have been okay as a child but not a great long-term quality when you're an adult.

All of this emotional competence, I believe, can only be done by recounting memories of the past that seem to be more memorable than others.

Try to read this book with an open mind and relate as much of it as possible to your own experiences. I seem to have my own emotions about certain situations, which may not be the same that you may have experienced, but I believe there is a relationship between it all. Something deeper. I hope to find out a little more about myself and hope you can figure out a little more about yourself too.

I don't know about you, but I've never been a human before. I don't know what to expect when my emotions arise, nor have I perfected my reactions to them. This life is about learning, not about knowing.

Although, learning is a cycle you should give back to. Once you have learned something, you should teach it. By teaching it you will learn even more about it and be more knowledgeable about the topic. *You should never stop learning.* Even if you happen to already know something, give yourself the opportunity to go over it again, and see what you missed.

Emotions are the same way. Just because you know the difference between the right and wrong responses or, when to be happy and sad, doesn't mean you know how to act in an appropriate manner, or deal with your responses correctly. Seriously, do you think every emotional response you have had has been accurate? Have you ever laughed jokingly over someone else's sad situation in hopes of cheering them up? I guess a better question is, are you sure you've chosen the right emotion to convey in every situation of your life? Probably not.

You have to fully understand the origin of where your emotions arise before you can gain control over them. You have a story that you're telling yourself daily, that leads to your social interactions in this world. It may not be the story that everyone else sees. Make sure your story is in sync with everyone around you. Be present in each moment and give your full undivided attention so you can be emotionally ready in any response you give.

What are our emotions

Let's take a look at some of the ideals I have around emotions, and how I try to analyze them by using my previous life experiences. First, I wanted to find a flow of how emotions are related. Emotions don't just come about, do they? They are triggered by some external source, right? I've noticed that they are usually triggered by someone interacting with us or our interactions with our surroundings. You don't just all of a sudden become irrationally angry at a flower for no reason, do you?

These external sources are experienced by, and interacted with, our five physical senses, and interpreted by our sixth sense, our mind. I will point out that I refer to a feeling as something that can be collected into an emotion. Multiple feelings can give way to your emotions. Your feelings are no more than your opinion or thoughts around a situation or object. See I believe, your emotion is an action that you project into the world about your feelings over something. Your feelings are your thoughts and opinions about your world. Got it? Great.

For instance, when you tell someone that they've hurt your feelings, what did they actually hurt? In actuality, and in the majority of the situations out there, you've simply disagreed with their thoughts and opinions because you perceive things differently. I call that being butt hurt. You're just angry or sad because someone doesn't agree with you. No one actually hurt you intentionally.

Although, I will recognize that there really is a way to hurt someone's feelings. That's usually through verbal and physical abuse. There is a difference between not liking what someone says, and someone belittling because they feel superior.

These are just some of the ways of how I interpret the meanings behind the words, feelings and emotions. I don't care for formal definitions so please do not fact check me. I will be the first to tell you that perception holds more weight than the truth in today's world. Once people have a perception of you, or of something, it doesn't matter what the truth is.

To expand more about feelings and emotions, let's try to understand where they come from.

Our mind puts together the positive, negative and neutral senses about something, which flows into a feeling about that person, object or place in time. These feelings turn into our state of emotion that we project into the world. This process begins when we are faced with what our senses input, though external sources like, your sense of sound, sight, touch, smell and taste. Some feelings that we get, we interpret to be pleasant, and we tend to want more of that sensation. This positive sensation can lead to wanting it all the time or wanting what others have and consuming ourselves with this object or place and stopping at nothing until we obtain it!

I classify these feelings of emotion into greed and envy. Although, it can be argued that the pleasant feeling could result in happiness or hope. I will touch more on my perception of these emotions and my outlook on them in the following chapters by going over my own personal experience with those emotions.

One thing to realize when you're in a state of emotional indecision, just because the voice in your head is telling you one thing, also known as your thoughts or feelings, that doesn't mean you should be feeling that way emotionally in the world. Thoughts are just that, they are ideas of how things may work or how they might be. That's not exactly how it is and may not be factual every time when it comes to how you should feel emotionally. With practice, we should be able to control our emotional decisions and responses. If you allow yourself enough time to question your thoughts before you react, you should be able to take charge of your emotional response. Right?

For instance, If I'm in a situation where someone says something and my thoughts tell me that I should disagree and be either angry or sad because of the scenario going on around me, that doesn't mean that I should act or feel that way. That is just a proposal of how I should feel when faced with that scenario. I have a choice to listen and believe my thoughts, or to rationalize if that's the best choice I should be making. Maybe I should be asking questions to the individual so I can make a more informed decision of how I should be feeling?

The process of internally analyzing your thoughts should give you enough time to respond appropriately to them. Just because the thoughts are there, doesn't mean you have to do what they say.

You have a consciousness that goes beyond the thoughts in your head. And those conscious decisions overrule all thought. Your consciousness is who you are. Your thoughts are an extraction. To be able to think and analyze is in a sense, a lab where you can run through scenarios and find a rational outcome. It is your consciousness that puts those thoughts into action. It is the final decision maker in the process of interacting in this world.

Your consciousness is who you are. It is your being. To be, is to be conscious. If you *just be* and not live by your thoughts, then you might free yourself from all burdens of emotional distress. If you're listening to your thoughts and are agreeing with them, then you might as well take any stranger's advice when given.

Hell, you might be safer listening to a stranger than your agreeable soft ass thoughts. Your thoughts will agree with you 100 percent of the time. That voice in your head that you use to reason with, wants to be right no matter if it makes you happy or sad. It just wants to be the one that's correct.

Let's use this example to expand more on this theory. Imagine, you're obsessing over some thought you have. Like being hopeful that you get an award or recognition for all the hard work you've been doing at your job. You feel like you deserve recognition, for all the time you've spent busting your ass. You start obsessing over all the different outcomes, on whether you'd get a promotion and what you would say when you received it. What if you don't get it? Will you continue to put in all the long hours of hard work? Will the voice in your head be angry and want retaliation?

Now imagine that there's this other voice in your head that takes a step back from you pondering all the possible outcomes of getting the recognition you've been working so hard for, and it starts to rationalize over what you're thinking about and questioning if you should even be obsessing about getting recognition for all your hard work. What part of you is aware that you are thinking at that moment? Think about that!

That could possibly be your consciousness determining if your thoughts are relative to what action needs to be taken or if an action needs to be taken at all. The likely solution would be to stop obsessing over the outcome and deal with the future when it happens.

You're not living in the future so why worry about it. Handle it, when the time comes. Focus on the present and the future will be shaped by your current actions. Don't let your feelings decide your actions or emotional response to objects in your world. Just get shit done and move on. Why obsess? You have to get over yourself at some point.

Another way of looking at the connection of your thoughts or feelings and your consciousness is to imagine that you're gazing at a beautiful scenery of a remarkable sunset over snowcapped mountains while taking a deep breath of fresh air. There are no thoughts running through your head while you're in that moment. You are essentially taking in all the wonders of the scenery, while living in that instance. All the colors. All the trees. All the clouds. You're in a state of flow.

When put into that situation do you think you would talk to yourself in your head about what colors there are and the shapes and sizes of those clouds or that they are even clouds at all or about how beautiful the sunset is compared to past sunsets? No!

You are consciously observing beauty in an unspoken but understandable and coherent manner, without words. Give it a try one day and observe your actions. Did you tell yourself about the scenery in your head or did you just consciously enjoy the speck of life you were a part of?

How is all of this possible

It is your consciousness that has this way about it, and it does not need words for interpretation. Our thoughts give us words and build context around objects for our ability to relate what we see in similar instances. Your consciousness on the other hand understands the present. It doesn't need the past to correlate how this is similar to another instance when you were looking at some beautiful scenery and were awestruck. You don't have to think about it. You know it. It is in your nature. You are essentially *being*.

The same method applies when you're in certain scenarios and may or may not agree with what's being said or being done. Your mind starts to recollect past experiences so they can be correlated with the present event in a way of determining how you should respond with emotion. If you live in that present moment and are just *being*, then you shouldn't be overtaken by your thoughts and how they think you should feel. You are just present.

To convey your feelings, your real raw emotion, you must only be present. Be present without thinking. Without thinking of doubt, thinking of future happiness or thinking of the mistakes of the past. You can't control when and why you think but for the sake of living, just *be* long enough in the present that you feel, without judgment of consequence. Feel the present as it happens without comparing it to the past or analyzing how it will affect your future. You will obtain authenticity and possibly, be happier with life.

I know I sound crazy but there are people in this world thinking the same way I think. They may not convey the scope or method the same, but the process is still similar. What I believe is that we have two parts to how we process information. We have this control plane process, which is our voiceless consciousness and a data plane process, which is our very loud and annoying thoughts. Both have a purpose and work in conjunction to spew out our actions into the world.

I think that your consciousness is the form of control in your life, and not your thoughts. The functions of your senses are how the data plane inputs and outputs information from and by decisions of your consciousness.

The control plane has authority over yes/no decisions, but the data plane takes in all the info and processes it, so it can get a resolution from the control plane, which in turn spits out an answer, so it can be passed along the path it should take. Whether it's a smile or a slap across someone's face, it all has to do with what data you take in and what the control plane says to do with it.

The control plane is the source of truth for the data plane. It's your morals. The data plane relies on the control plane for the final decision-making process for all the data it receives before it sends its response out into the world. If the data plane gets corrupt or stops working all together, the control plane would misunderstand what it receives and may send out bad information. Garbage in garbage out. Do you know anyone who may have this problem?

If one of your five senses are off, you may misinterpret the data you're taking in and end up not matching the proper control plane decision, to the actual facts you gathered. If your eyes think the sky is falling then you may consciously think it's the end of the world when in fact, your blood pressure may have just crashed and you're about to pass out.

Let's expand on my theory and take into account looking at a map before navigating through a town. You use your eyes to read and to figure out which roads you have to traverse to get to your destination, right? After you study the map for a while, plotting your path and taking down all the names of the streets you have to take, you set the map down and start on your course.

While you're navigating, you might end up taking a wrong turn due to not reading a street name properly. You may have interpreted Platt Street for Plant Street. Your sense of sight misinterpreted the data your control plane needed to make a crucial decision in your course and led you in the wrong direction. You can obviously correct your course by checking the data again, but more carefully this time, and you'll end up at your destination, as planned.

How about another example. You're in a conversation with a friend and you're talking about people and their pets. Your friend happens to mention that they can't stand cat people but also didn't realize you owned a cat. Now, you definitely heard them correctly and didn't misinterpret them, but you've taken their comment personally. You feel butt hurt by their statement.

Although their comment was a general statement about cat owners who have 5 or more cats and knit personal jackets for all their kittens. Your friend doesn't actually dislike you because you have a cat. Your thoughts disrupted the information it received and almost had you respond in a negative manner. That's not a good thing. Again, garbage in garbage out.

The point here is, it's easy to take in the wrong data for analysis to be compared with your source of truth. If your data is corrupt, you will make the wrong decision because what you believe to be true is not actually a fact, but rather an opinion and you might end up throwing your hot coffee in your friend's face that just talked shit about you and your cat.

Make sure your decisions are coming from the right place and not the random thoughts that pester your consciousness. When you feel you've started to take things personally, ask questions, because you may have a little butt hurt bubbling up.

Also, as I mentioned earlier, if your source of truth is wrong then you will also have corrupt data which could lead you to spreading falsehoods or misinformation. You will not take the right path per say or may even blurt out something that is assumed to be true.

With your control plane and data plane split into two parts but still reliant on each other, you have to question, is that all we have? If the control plane is the source of truth for all decisions and the data plane is there for collecting data for analysis to be sent to that control plane for that decision, how can you short cut some of the *knowns* that don't have to be scrutinized as much?

Take the example from earlier of looking at the beautiful scenery of a sunset over snowcapped mountains. You do not have to analyze the colors or shapes. You just know them, right? A tree is a tree. The sun is yellow. You don't have to question what it is or what color it is. You know it, without words. This is called cut-through processing. It's already familiar and known so there is no thinking involved by the data plane. It simply passes the responses through.

Now on the other hand if it's something you have not encountered before, like the first time seeing the mountains, or an alien spaceship which would be cool to see, your brain does this store-and-forward process where it collects the new data, processes it for relevant information and response, then stores it in the control plane as a source of truth to be compared to at a future time.

I will say one thing about my view of the world and how I interpret my interactions, it's abstract. I'm an odd dude. Everything I just went through about my reasoning of how I analyze the creation of emotions and how we operate as humans, is due to my profession. I work in Information Technology and relate a lot about what human life is, to the functionality of the computers I work on every day.

Those last examples of control-plane, data-plane, cut-through and store-and-forward are forms of computer network processing. Guess who just learned a little about computer networking and how data is passed through devices on the Internet? You did! Never stop learning.

I'm sure after you read this book you probably wouldn't have thought the person who wrote this book had a background in computer networking but rather some sort of psychology degree or just some random idiot on a rant.

Since you don't have the option to ask me anything, you'll have to read on to find out more about me, and form your own opinion. I may be odd, but I'm interesting.

Why is this important

Sometimes the best way to understand people is to ask questions. The more you are able to find out from asking questions, the less you will assume. In your day-to-day life, be sure to ask the important questions to those you interact with so you don't collect the wrong data.

Ask questions like, who were they before you knew them? Are they the type of cat person who knits their kitties coats? Who did they want to be when they grew up? And, who are they now? Did they see themselves as an obsessive cat person? Don't judge. Just ask.

You think you know someone, but you don't. You don't know where they've been and the situations they've been in, do you? Have you lived their life and felt what they felt? You may know some of the situations they've been through if you were there, but you don't know the whole story. You don't know what's going on in their head. I bet you barely know yourself.

When is the last time you've cataloged the events in your life? Have you asked yourself any of the questions I just mentioned? Who were you when you were growing up? Do you like cats so much that you'd make them their own coats? Who did you want to be when you grew up? Are you what you envisioned you'd be now? Have you gone through your memories and written down the events that stand out to you, then analyzed them to understand why you did what you did in your past? Probably not. Why would you do something like that in the first place?

I asked myself that same question when I started the idea of this book. Who would want to read about my thought processes and my view of life anyways? Well, me for one. I truly wanted to recap what I've been through. Some things made it in the book and others are not ready for prime time, but I did have time to reflect back on it all and realized, I'm a fucking idiot. I know what I've done, and I have no regrets. I'll own up to it all, if it's true.

I will say, I wouldn't trade this process of laying down my thoughts for you to scrutinize, for anything. I can finally own up to what my past has turned me into and look forward to what I can change in the future. By analyzing my life, I can be more authentic. With authenticity I can act with integrity towards others and be accountable for my actions and words.

If you feel like something is off in your world and your emotions are running your life, I would suggest a great way to regain control in your life is to start digging into *who you were.* Do this by going back through conversations that you have had throughout a day, or parts of your life, and analyze them. Question your decisions in those moments.

When you go through what you have said or have done in the past, and critique everything, you are going through a process of sharpening your sword so you can be better prepared in the future.

Have you ever heard the saying that the sharpest sword is the tongue? I'm sure you've also heard that the pen is mightier than the sword, but just because the pen is perceived to be less dangerous or lethal than the sword, doesn't mean the pen cannot do just as much damage. Because it can. The pen rather just happens to have more control over what you convey versus the sword.

I believe the sword in the previous analogy is your tongue. You see, with a pen you have a chance to strike things from the record, and in a way, be more in control. You can even toss what you've written down aside and into the trash for no one to ever know it was ever written. But once words have left your tongue, the sword, there is no taking it back. Once it is said, it has been said. Once others have heard it, it cannot be unheard.

This is why the saying, the pen is mightier than the sword, holds weight. You have control over what leaves your being when you're able to write it down. You have the opportunity to reduce your emotional response by taking time to articulate your words. It's not so easy when you start firing off at the mouth.

The point is to keep your sword sharp. If it is swung wildly, it has the ability to cut off one's ear. Rather, keep it in its sheath and only pull it out when there is an opportunity to strike. Make damn sure you use it wisely or you will fall on deaf ears.

Now that I have used my pen to convey my intentions of this book, clear as mud I'm sure, let's carry on with learning a little more about me, and where I come from. Maybe things will all fall into place, if I start from the beginning…

Part One:

In the beginning

Chapter 2

I AM WHO I AM

These two phrases. "Who I am!" and "Who am I?"
are very entangled. Both are one doubt away from each
other. Have you told yourself that's just "Who I am!" and
then doubtfully asked, "Who am I?" It's a double-edged
sword and you better be confident enough to have the
answer before doubt creeps in.

By going through the process of writing this book I've
had the opportunity to go through this exercise of
wondering, or better yet questioning, who I really was. It
was a long process. To understand "Who I am", I had to
understand where I had been. Like most things, if you're
able to reverse engineer the object you will figure out
why it is the way it is. You can also better understand
how it works and also how to improve upon it later.

Same can be said for your life. You happen to be in the
present state of your own product today but if you want to
know how you got to be where you are, all you have to

do is go back to the beginning. You have to reverse engineer your life.

As I started to process my past to find out who I am today, I had to determine the facts of what I am now and how I got here, so I can answer the question of why I am the way I am today.

Here's some background notes on what I am at this moment. I'm a young adult in my mid 30's that has become frightfully aware of everything around myself. I have an engineer's brain and I want to find the meaning behind everything I interact with. I literally question everything every second of the day.

The most recent conundrum that has plagued my brain is "What the hell am I doing here? I am a human on a giant rock in the middle of an extremely vast universe. How did that happen?" and "Why am I where I am today, physically and professionally?". Those are very difficult questions to answer. It's almost an unsolvable problem. The harder the problem the better I say. By nature, I am a problem solver. I feel as though I've been raised in this manner but maybe I was born with it.

When I reached first grade, I got put into an advanced class where my problem-solving skills would be nurtured. Someone saw something in me and thought it'd be good to enhance those skills. In that advanced class, we were given things to solve like puzzles and other games that took brain power to figure out. I stayed in those classes all through elementary.

Even today I still like to learn about the inner workings of the objects in our lives and solve problems. I made for a natural engineer. No matter what discipline I would have fallen into as an adult, I would have turned into some sort of engineer.

It's because I like to search for questions to ask so I can find all the answers to all of life's obstacles. For instance, "Why does that move like that?", "How does that grow in those conditions?", "What kind of reactions will be the effect of these actions?". Those are just a few questions I ponder about every day of my life. I am curious and want to understand the answers to all those questions. I guess that's who I am from a personality perspective, which is only one perceived aspect of myself. I've come to find, there is always more than what's on the surface of the first answer. There is a deeper meaning behind everything. That's at least what I believe. Nothing in life is as it is first perceived.

I've always had this way of thinking. Maybe not as analytical as I am today but even when I was a little boy, I stood back and observed situations. I was the quiet kid who never engaged in activities or conversations unless provoked. One of the main reasons was from the fear of being made fun of because I was so awkward and shy. I sat around watching everyone else play and have fun. It was a way of learning for me.

I guess I tried to figure out what others were doing and why it was so important to them. Just to learn from people. Maybe I needed to act in the same way? As a kid, I'd ask myself as I observed others; "What is the purpose of playing tag?", "Why are you happy that that kid just gave you a piece of grass?", "Why is that kid crying?", "Why am I crying?". I never really tried to figure it out when I was that age. I was too young to grasp the reasoning behind the emotions or the context of one's actions towards another individual. I just sat quietly observing and taking in all the information.

Hopefully I'm not alone in questioning everything in life but that maybe you too have also imagined yourself sitting there pondering those same questions as I have my entire life. Maybe you don't know how to navigate this world either? I had no idea how social interactions were supposed to work or how I was supposed to act as a child. Shit, I still don't know how to act in public to this day. I'm an idiot when it comes to social interactions.

As I grew older and into adulthood, I'm still an observer of people and creatures of this Earth. I contemplate all the mysteries of this life. Some mysteries I have solved, like enjoying craft beer and making hot sauce. I'll save that knowledge for later and share it in a book you can rest on your coffee table. Other mysteries are of a spiritual nature that give me peace, but I may never truly solve them.

Even if I have been able to figure out some of the simpler truths of the material or spiritual life, I still know what I am not. I am not a literary genius, nor do I possess any background in literature. I am not a writer or for that matter very good at spelling and grammar. I will create fragmented sentences and run on sentences that run on forever and ever. I have only claimed to be a dumb ol' country boy from a once not so known town in Mississippi. I also don't know nothing. Yes, I know that's a double negative. Wink wink!

To know more about who I am, or more or less who I am not, I am not a runner. I'm sure you bought this book thinking it was all about running and how to be a better runner. Well, sorry to disappoint but this isn't a book about running. I'm not going to outline how to prepare for running races or anything like that because hell I don't know how to do that myself. After reading it you're probably not going to be a better runner, maybe, but not likely. This also isn't a book that's intentionally about Psychology or Emotional Intelligence. I don't know shit about that either. Oh, I also cuss a lot if you haven't noticed. I'm an extremely emotional person and I use passionate words to describe my feelings.

I may curse a lot to convey my feelings towards subjects but that doesn't mean you should be offended. If I offend you, I hope it's from the topic or some performance I gave that disgusted you. We don't need curse words solely to offend people. We can do a great job of that from our interactions with people from our out of control emotions. To each their own but to each own they shall reap.

What does it take to survive

As I mentioned previously, I grew up in a small town in Mississippi. I didn't mention I have two older brothers who liked to use me as a punching bag when we were kids. When I was younger you can guarantee I got my daily beat down by my two older brothers. It was all fun and games until one of us got hurt.

All of that rough housing made me partly who I am today. Seeing as my crying was conveyed to me as a problem and a sign of weakness by my brothers, I learned to bury my emotions and not cry as much. I toughened up quickly and learned to fight back or just run and hide when I couldn't overcome the situation. All techniques are survival skills when you have older brothers. You have to be tough when you're the youngest in the family. I learned walking away was the best resolution to any situation. It takes a lot of strength to walk away.

I'm analytical by nature as I noted before, but I honed that skill even more from all the battles I was in with my brothers. For instance, when I was faced with the situation of being held down on the ground in a figure four by one of my brothers, I usually thought to myself, "How can I get out of this situation?", I would try everything until something worked. I took note of what didn't work but more importantly what I did that got me out of that situation. I never wanted to give up. I was willing to have my arm broken rather than to give in to these guys. I wanted nothing more than to get out of the martial art hold they had me in and prove how tough I was. My problem-solving brain was in full effect and working at top speed in those intense situations. That led to improving how well I could find a solution in the most stressful of times. Cool heads usually prevail.

As time passed, I started to slip out of most of the holds and stand my ground, but not for long. Somehow as we grew older, my brothers got bigger while I stayed the same size? Strange indeed. It could have been some of my recreational activities? No one may ever know but science.

My brothers are twice my size now and can throw a hefty punch. Needless to say, I never really won any wrestling matches and I'm okay with that. I will probably never win or gain the upper hand when it comes to wrestling my brothers. That's alright by me. I know my threshold.

As a child I had to overcome a lot of adversity like being the youngest of three and not letting things get me down. Losing to my brothers during knock down drag out wrestling events really motivated me to try harder but that wasn't my only influence as a kid. I got picked on at school a lot too. I guess I was the strange kid that had a look to him that said, "Hey, come fuck with me." I took whatever was given to me and had to overcome it all. Yes, I will note I usually cried and went in any corner I could find so I could pout but I eventually grew out of it.

As children we are fairly resilient as long as we have someone in our lives who helps us to see the brighter side of life. I turned out okay, but I had a wonderful positive influence from my mother. Love you Mom!

Whether it was my brothers who verbally or physically put me down or kids at school who would point and laugh and call me names, I always tried to keep my head held high. I knew that if I showed weakness that it would only bring more pain.

As for my two brothers, thank you for molding me into someone who doesn't take shit from anyone, I love you guys too!

I was a quiet kid for the most part and tried to keep to myself but there were a few times when I got my butt whooped at school. I was pretty much a loner as a child. I sat back and distanced myself from others. I didn't have the self-esteem that made me an outgoing person. I was an outsider. I didn't care to interact with other people. I was the type of kid who liked to sit back and keep to himself. I just didn't understand how to be normal like other kids and didn't know how to fit in. I was never good at making friends either. The only friends I ever made were because they befriended me first.

Looking back at those days, I can say I learned a lot about people and how to discern which ones would turn out to be good individuals just by their interactions with others.

Think of the people you have come to know from your past. Which ones were bullies and how did they turn out? Did they come across a life changing event or did they turn out exactly like you would have thought? What about those likable kids? Did they become super successful and cool, or did they become average people with a mediocre life?

You will never know a person until you've walked in their shoes for their entire life. You don't know what's going on in their head. The way you perceive them may not be how they turn out in the future. Be nice to everyone because you never know when you may need their help. What goes around comes around. Don't step on the toes of some ass you're going to have to kiss in the future.

You never know what someone else is going through. Their day may be shittier than yours. Speak softly and deliver your statements with neutrality.

When I was a teenager and hit puberty, a flood of emotions opened up. People joke about it and will warn you, but you never know until you experience it for yourself. That's true about most things but especially true about puberty. With puberty you become a human lost in a sea of feelings about yourself and what other people's perceptions are of you. That can be a difficult time and could be detrimental if you do not have the right support structure around you like a reliable family member or close friends that are truly there for your benefit and not theirs.

There were times where I got so damn depressed that I just wanted to kill myself. It was usually over a girl or a conflict with a friend. A lot of the friends that I had were not there for my benefit either. They were there for their own and most likely wanting something from me to benefit them. Half the time it was the same girl I was after. I guess most teenagers go through that time in their lives. I pray that they make it out alive. For those who are contemplating ending it all over something stupid, like a girl, don't. Find someone to talk to. Anyone. People in this world do not know how to deal with their emotions. Especially teenagers! They have no idea what they're doing. They get overwhelmed and overtaken easily by despair. Especially on social media. This, sadly, usually leads to suicide and mass murders.

I can see why people commit suicide though. This is a fucked up world we live in. Some stupid shit is going on by the smartest beings colonizing this planet.

I have many times thought to commit suicide because I was done with this society we've created. My whole life I have wanted my life to end because I was fed up with all the bullshit that beats us down, but I haven't had the courage to go through with the process. Maybe I'm just crazy enough to enjoy the madness this life surprises us with? I truly want to see this life through to the end. I want to know what we are capable of as a whole. Humans are smart but damnit we can be dumb as shit. Would we really start to drop bombs that could kill everyone on

Earth? Would we really start a chemical war because we don't like someone? How petty. I think I'll stay awhile and see what the future holds. I mean really, what's the worst that can happen? I could die!

Though I'll admit, I've not only thought about checking out of life, but I've attempted it many times before. At one point as a young teen, I tried to go through with hurting myself because I thought there was no other way out. I had the worst life ever. If you have children, I'm sure you've heard them say "This is the worst day EVER!", "I want out of this world", or "I hate my life". It's ok. They will get over it, but you need to be there for them and lift them up. Otherwise, they may take an unreasonable action that you're not going to like.

Always nurture your children and be there for them when no one else will. Being a kid or teenager is difficult. Hopefully you remember how you were and can relate to them. You remember the times when you needed a friend or someone to talk to, right? Don't you think you should take action in those times that your kids may be going though? They may try to hurt themselves. It can happen and often does.

Now, even though I attempted to end my life a few times when I was younger, I wasn't brave enough to cut myself or do real damage when I was discouraged. I was scared of the outcome. I didn't know what would happen after the fact. I was scared of death but also wanted it.

I did try falling off the top bunk of my bunk bed to break an arm once. I thought to myself if I was lucky, I could possibly break my neck and get some attention but after a few failed attempts of doing that, I realized how bad it hurt and thought that was a pretty stupid idea. Praise be to God that I didn't break anything, or worse.

I'm glad I made it through those dark times in my life as a teen. Some situations felt as though I only had one option at hand. I think what's more important to recognize is that even though I felt like I only had one option, in reality I just wanted to escape from my problems that I created.

Running away from your emotions is the only way to get rid of them, right?

I will note that most of those dark times were over a girl. Damn they can get into your head. Don't let that happen to you. It's never worth it. There is so much more to life than to have one person get inside your head and play games with you. Fuck that noise!

After having those episodes of suicidal thoughts as a teen, I was so depressed about feeling that way in the first place. I feel lucky to have made it through unharmed but more than anything, I felt stupid for acting in such a way that would have changed the course of my life into something inconceivable. I really am stupid, but aren't we all? We never seem to see past the present moment.

We always have these choices we can make. We can go left, or we can go right. We can do good, or we can do bad. We're always fighting with ourselves in a constant struggle on how we should deal with our emotions. Sometimes we get lucky and something stops us from going too far in the wrong direction. Sometimes, not.

Whether you choose to go left or to go right, make sure it keeps you moving forward. Choose the path forward and not the one that walks you backwards. Don't stand still either. Make the choice for love over hate. Right over wrong. Living over dying.

How to play the game

Life is like a game of chess. There are pieces that you can control and advance them as you see fit but there are pieces you cannot control. The point of chess is to advance the pieces in a way that you gain the upper hand and put your opponent into check.

In life your opponent is that voice in your head that sympathizes with every decision you make that keeps you safe. It wants you to lose so it can be right.

You must be smart in the game of chess. You must predict not only your next move but your opponent's next move. You have to play many steps ahead of the one you're on. This game of life is full of strategy. You must plan your next moves carefully and cautiously anticipate the outcome of that move and what your opponent may do to stop you from progressing. You need to find a move that takes you forward. Even if it is one step forward and two steps left.

Yes, you may lose a game here and there, but this game of life is a very long one. You must have patience and keep score. You never know, you may end up winning in the end depending on how you classify winning. Best 300,000 out of 500,000?

I've been a loser my whole life. I've lost more than I've won. That doesn't stop me from getting up and fighting for that one win that changes the course of my life. That single win out of a hundred thousand loses, is always worth the fight. So yes, I am a loser and I will always be a loser. Not because I suck at what I do but because I challenge myself with things I've never attempted. I accept I'm going to lose when I start. The more you branch out to explore this world, the more it will beat you down. But if you get up when you get knocked down, you'll learn how to play better in the next match. Regardless of how many times you lose or fail at your attempt to gain ground, you have to learn not to make that move again. You should at least start to predict an outcome from your previous actions. Cause and effect, they call it.

We can all be fortune-tellers in the sense of predicting probable outcomes. The best usually learns from their past games. Practice makes perfect.

Think about how many times a master chess player has lost in their past to become a Grandmaster. I'm sure they had to learn from their mistakes. I can probably bet that they took note of some of their competitor's moves too. Use your past, and even others past experiences as your advantage in progressing each chess piece one move at a time.

Another way to learn how to become the best of the best is to talk to people. I mentioned this earlier, but you have to ask people questions. That's how you learn.

Make acquaintance with them so you can continue to learn from the life they've led. If you never reach out to learn or try to get better, you'll never know anything better than what you currently know. You will not know what else is out there and all the endless possibilities that can be achieved that could lead to your success in life.

You have to be the change that makes the first move or at least a move that keeps you in the game. It's your action and your involvement that is going to get you somewhere. If you lay stagnant and don't make any moves, you will not move forward. There will be no progress. You will not be successful.

When do you wake up

As a teenager there was a lot of change and progression in my life, but I wasn't always moving forward. I was just learning how to play this game of life. I was awkward and weird. I wasn't that kid who knew how to deal with his emotions yet, or for that matter, how important your emotions are in your life.

While a teenager I still kept to myself but sometimes I would make a public appearance and embarrass myself. I didn't hang out with the "cool" kids nor did I hang out with the nerds. I wasn't into sports or even band for that matter. Although I liked sports and played baseball when I was a kid, I didn't play any as a teenager. I stopped playing baseball once I got beaned in the head by a fast ball in little league. Maybe that's what's wrong with me?

I was in the "in-between crowd". Being this inbetweener primarily consisted of smoking, skateboarding, dying my hair, wearing dark clothes and just being weird. We were too good to be cool and not smart enough to be a nerd. It was great to have friends with commonalities. We had our social activity, which was well, smoking and terrorizing the neighborhood.

I wasn't in any after-school activities either. No, I mostly hung out with my friends and smoked. That carried on for a few years and eventually my academic grades in high school became not so great. I skipped a lot of school and didn't really care about anything. I was falling into darkness. I didn't give any emotional thought into my actions, words or interactions between anybody. I was living in a fog, a fog of idiocy.

This phase of my life as an inbetweener was my outlet for the mundane life in a small town in the countryside of Mississippi. What else is there to do in a small town? Seriously! Cow tipping?

Midway into high school, I thought I knew everything. Except I really didn't. I'm sure you can relate. You probably thought highly of yourself too. School came second to my extracurricular activities. I missed a lot of days of school. I lived right next door to it too! I really had no excuse for missing school unless I was deathly ill.

Skipping school was easy in high school. I would start walking to school in the morning and just keep walking past it to my buddy's house who lived a block on the other side of the school. We didn't do much but the usual, smoke, hang out and watch TV.

Because of those actions of skipping school and not putting in the work, I barely graduated high school. For the most part, I did the bare minimum to pass all through high school. I was okay with that for some reason. I was smart but I could care less about straight A's. Most of my previous years in school were all advanced classes that focused on building up my problem solving and analytical skills but once I got to high school, I made sure I wasn't in any advanced classes. I wanted to have fun and breeze through school. Looking back, that was a poor decision.

What poor decisions have you made in your past that you regret? Did they change you for the better or for the worse? Have you owned up to them yet?

We all have the ability to correct our actions even if we don't do anything about them at that time because if you never do anything about your mistakes, they will stay mistakes. I have a few that I still regret and am trying to figure out what I should do about them besides accepting it and moving forward. That may very well be the only thing I can actually do.

I continued living my teenage years as an idiot until my senior year in high school. It was the end of the first semester of my senior year and my grades were not good to say the least. Before the winter break a guidance counselor contacted my mother and informed her of how poor my grades were. Well, they were okay in all areas but English class. Yes, they were low, but I thought I was still passing in English. I thought I was smart. I had planned to only do enough to pass each class every year, but my senior year would not be like years past.

When the guidance counselor said that I was failing English, she portrayed it as if I didn't have a chance in hell to graduate high school. She said I would have to go to summer school if I wanted to graduate. That meant no graduation ceremony, and for some reason that got to me. I had always envisioned graduating and walking across that stage with my classmates. It messed with me pretty bad.

I felt stupid after being informed I wasn't going to graduate but I didn't think I was that bad off. Let's call it a miscalculation on my part. One I would vow to never make again.

The guidance counselor, as negative as she was, informed me that summer school wasn't the only way that I could graduate. There was one other way but there wasn't much hope for me in achieving it. If I wanted to graduate with my classmates and join in on the graduation ceremony, I would have to make a 95 and above on every essay, test or project. Yes, there wasn't much hope for me to graduate in the normal school year. I was destined for summer school. That is, if I didn't just give up and drop out like most of my friends had done. Seriously. Most all of my friends at that time had dropped out of school and either gotten their GED or were just working a normal trade job.

At the end of that first semester and during that winter break I had some time to digest what the guidance counselor told my mother and me. Let me tell you one thing, I got reminded of my situation daily by my mother. Thank you for that Mom!

I hated English class. It didn't help that I had the hardest English teacher at the school either. Regardless of all that negativity and excuses I gave myself, I knew I could overcome this obstacle in my life. No way was I going to lose. No way was I going to bow down to the challenge. I don't give up easily and this challenge was just what I needed. It was a wakeup call for sure. If I didn't win, I would be destined for a shitty life. At least that's what I told myself about my future if I didn't graduate.

There were things in my life that I had to change if I wanted to move forward. One of those things was what I did with my friends, smoking and fucking off. This meant less time with friends and more time studying.

Smoking as an everyday routine had me standing still. I was as stagnant as the smoke cloud that filled the room. Smoking was my hindrance that kept me from moving forward. There are also other habits in our daily routines that keep us down or that we don't think are harmful to us but ultimately keeps us from progressing. What keeps you down?

The same old shit I did day in and day out was not getting me anywhere. I had the challenge of graduating high school with my peers or flunking and going to summer school while everyone else partied. I had to change it up. I wanted to party too!

Sometimes we need challenges like that to keep us engaged in life. Without life's challenges we can become complacent and take things for granted. I especially was taking my ride through high school for granted and it bit me in the ass. I had a plan to overcome my shortcomings though.

I knew what I had to do, and I was serious. I quit playing around and acting like a kid. I gave up smoking and hanging out with friends at social events. I changed my appearance by wearing preppy clothes and cutting my hair. Those things were not going to get me the grade I needed to pass English but at least I looked the part. I studied hard. It was challenging for sure. I had my eyes set on the goal of graduating high school. But that's all it was, a goal. I needed that though because goals keep you moving forward. Without a goal or something to achieve, what are you living for?

Where do you start

The thing about goals is that you have to have a plan. Not only do you have to have a plan, but you have to put that plan into action. You can't just sit around talking about it. Nothing is going to happen. You have to actually go out and attack that plan. It takes force being applied to an object at rest to move it. Whatever your goal is, you have to make a plan and put it into action.

My mindset changed when faced against not graduating. I knew I had a problem that needed to be solved and my goal was to solve that problem. To get to a solution, I needed a plan. The plan was fairly simple. Quit doing dumb shit and study my ass off. Those two parts of my plan required my action towards them. If I had never acted on them, then I would have never attempted to graduate or achieve my goal that I set out to conquer. I would have taken what was given to me, which was summer school. Blah.

Life is full of those moments. You face an issue that you feel needs to be solved but for you to solve it you have to do something about it. Imagine this, you're sitting on your couch and you're hungry, but you don't want to move off the couch to actually go get something to eat. In that instance you have a choice. Remain hungry and pass out on the couch in hopes that it goes away. Maybe when you wake up, you'll have enough motivation to get up and go find food? Or, you get your ass up right then and there to go get some damn food. Quit being lazy!

Too many of us choose not to act on what we want in hopes that it will fix itself or go away. Well I'll tell you one thing; things don't always magically fix themselves. It takes someone willing to solve the problem through action to make it go away.

So, when you want change in your life just remember, you have to have a goal that has a plan of action tied to it but more importantly you have to get off your ass and put the plan into motion. It's logic people!

When the second semester of my senior year in high school started, I was a new person. I was clean cut and dressing preppy. I was engaged in my classes but more importantly, I stayed home and studied instead of fucking off. I didn't skip any more classes or go jerk around with my friends. I hit the books and put in the time. By mid-semester my grades were improving in all my classes but especially in my English class. I was doing what everyone thought couldn't be done. I was making 95 and above on all my assignments in English. When no one believed I could do it, I believed in myself.

But I knew I couldn't let my accomplishments lead to my failure either. I didn't give myself credit for what I had done because I knew I had a couple months left of busting my ass. I kept up all the good work I was doing and when it came to finals, I was ready. But was I ready to make a 95+ on my final exam in English?

Well, I did. It was tough but I didn't give in and listen to the naysayers. I stayed the course until the end. I didn't celebrate early. I didn't let anything distract me or discourage me. My hard work paid off and I won the battle. I graduated high school, barely, and coasted into Summer for some time off before I had to become an adult because we all know I had shit grades and wouldn't be getting a full ride into college.

Chapter 3

Preparing for life as an adult

Once summer ended and I was officially an 18-year-old adult, I got a job. A grown-up job! One of my friends got me the job as the summer was ending. There was a lot of responsibility that came along with that job and also, a lot of independence. This job taught me a ton about how to be a man and how to work hard. That attitude and discipline came from my boss. He was an awesome person who was tough as nails and smart as a whip. A cowboy for sure.

I was a low voltage cable installer. Doesn't sound interesting, I know. The thing about the role I was in was that I had to travel 100% of the time. I spent most days driving across the country from town to town installing data and voice cabling. With the aspect of traveling, I learned to branch out into the world and outside of the comfort zone of my hometown. It was a pivotal point in my life and I never really realized how much that job changed me for the better. But that job didn't last long.

I screwed it up by getting a DUI charge a few months into it. The charges got dropped but nonetheless, it was a valuable lesson learned. *Don't do stupid things that draw attention to yourself.* Take that wisdom and stick it in your pocket as a life lesson. I'm serious.

After dealing with the court system, I decided to go another path in my career and not travel as much. So, I found another job in my hometown at a deli. Call it fate but this second job I got out of high school was the best thing that had ever happened to me.

That's when I met my now Wife. I couldn't have ever imagined that anyone could love me like she has. To be honest, I had never before been treated as she had treated me. She showed me a whole new world of love and got me to change my childish ways. I needed to grow up and she was my compass. We all need to "Man up" at some point and she let me do that in a subtle way, and on my own terms. She nudged me in the right direction and allowed me to believe in myself but also believe in others. She knew that anything was possible and that I could do anything as long as I put forth the effort. I trusted her, and still do.

Meeting her was literally the best thing that has ever happened to me.

With this job at the deli and a new romance, I had a lot more time to think about my future than ever before. I wasn't traveling everyday trying to get from point A to point B. I was living a slower paced life. Just going through the motions as a young man learning how to be an adult in an ocean of love. Life was good.

As I grew older and into a young man entering into my twenties, I had an urge to do something important with my life. Yes, I was happy with where I worked but I questioned if that was what I really wanted to do as a career? This slower paced life felt as though I was standing still, and once again not making any progress. I realized I hadn't achieved anything since graduating except dodging a felony. I looked forward into the future to what my life would be if I had kept to the status quo and I didn't like the outcome. Same old shit day in and day out. I wasn't learning anything new nor was I on track to. How could I move forward if I was continually doing the same thing?

Well, I decided that there was one thing that could propel my life into full blown adulthood. I needed to go to college and apply myself. I needed to find something worth exploring and change up my routine. Working at the deli was good and all, but I knew I could do so much more. Before committing to college, I had gotten a second job at a packaging plant in the late hours of the night, before working at the deli in the morning just to make ends meet. Working part time didn't allow for much money to be used towards rent or anything else for that matter and especially college, but I made do.

While looking into college courses, I tried to find a career path that suited my personality and creativity. I randomly chose Mechanical Engineering. At the time it sounded interesting, but I had no idea what it was. I knew I was mechanically inclined and good at engineering, so I thought this college course was probably a good fit. Once I was able to apply for the classes and started college, I realized I was dead wrong. One semester in and I was done. If you don't know what Mechanical Engineering is, don't worry, someone out there does it for a living and knows it so you don't have to.

I changed my major to Automotive Engineering. I knew I would be interested in that and it would likely work out down the road when it came time to get a big boy job after college. And if it didn't, well, I would know how to fix my own car!

College reminded me of grade school. It was a great place to sit back and watch what everyone else was doing. In college I started to learn more about social interactions. More importantly I figured out what to do and what not to do as an adult, as well as when to speak and when not to speak. I also grasped the understanding of when I should engage my emotions over a topic or whether I should even participate in certain activities in class. Trust me, there are some things you do not want to raise your hand for, nor do you want to challenge the teacher on a topic they are passionate about. The outcome is probably going to be extra work. I know from experience. Remember my earlier life lesson about not drawing attention to yourself. Well that goes along with keeping your mouth shut. I still suck at that today but at least I know it's a flaw. Why is it so hard to not inform people of the truth or release your passionate opinions? I cannot let ignorance be spread!

Even if I don't know when to bite my tongue, I know when to put in effort and when not to. If I wanted to get through college, I best sit back and make sure I'm not involved in more than I could handle. I mean, I was working two jobs at that point and going to college at night. Do you think I had time for extra credit in class? Nope!

College didn't last long for me though. After changing majors from Mechanical to Automotive Engineering, I ended up having to drop out after a year and a half so I could get a fulltime job that paid more than I made at my two part-time jobs combined. I was forced, if you will, to grow up even more and learn accountability. The truth was, I had to move out of my Mom's house. This little birdy had to be pushed out of the nest.

To be honest, I needed to learn how to be an adult before figuring out what I wanted to do for a career. There was also the fact that I didn't have a vehicle to get to and from work anymore and needed to obtain another one. What happened? Oh, I totaled it around a concrete telephone pole. Luckily no one else was involved. I guess I had it coming.

What had happened was, I was overly exhausted and shouldn't have been driving. My normal routine was to go to night school at college, then head to work at my part-time job at the packing plant directly after class. After that I usually had a couple hours between that night job and my morning shift at the deli where I went home to get some food. On the morning of my accident, I should have taken a nap!

While leaving my house to go to the deli, I lost control of my vehicle in a curve right after a light rain shower. I spun around in a 180 and was heading backwards towards the opposite side of the road at 45 mile per hour. My rear tire hit the curb and flung my truck into the air. Which propelled me into a light pole. The force was enough to cause my vehicle to wrap around it and bend my SUV in half. It sucked.

I stumbled out of the vehicle while someone was screaming at me to lay down on the ground. I thought I was being arrested. To my avail, it was a stranger who had seen the accident and was worried for my life.

The guy called 911 and got an ambulance on the scene. I was dazed but not that bad off. I didn't feel hurt, and nothing was broken. Though, when the ambulance arrived, the EMTs persisted I get in the vehicle and take a ride to the hospital to get checked out. I agreed after looking at the damage to my truck. I'm not sure how I walked away from that wreck. Especially since I wasn't wearing a seatbelt. In retrospect, I'm glad that light pole was there. If it hadn't been, I would have barrel rolled my vehicle across an open field. I'm sure I would have been ejected from my vehicle and died.

A funny story about all of this is, once I was in the ambulance and we started to head to the hospital, the ambulance broke down not even 20 feet from the accident. Thank God I wasn't seriously injured! We had to wait a little while for another ambulance to transport me to the hospital. That joyous event gave me time to bitch and moan about the situation I was in but also contemplate what I was going to do with my life from then on.

When does one grow up

I was still taking the easy road in life and knew I needed to move out of my Mom's place. I wasn't growing up quick enough, I guess. So, after my wreck and getting a new vehicle, I found a fulltime job and quit college as planned. I started out on a new path. I bounced around every year renting a new house and even went through a few random workplaces.

The best knowledge in how to do something is experience doing it. Man did I learn a thing or two. One thing I learned was that I needed to keep track of how much money I had in the bank. Financial institutions charge a lot when you overdraw your account. If you're not tracking your money properly, you'll acquire a few charges that will sink you lower into debt.

For a few years, let's say 5, as I bounced around from house to house and job to job, I was spending the majority of my life with my now Wife. We were two young kids in love. She somehow put up with me and wanted to be with me all the time. Girls...

We fantasized about our lives together. Things like; how many kids we would have and what kind of house we would live in. All the while I was still figuring out what to do with my career so we could live out this fantasy.

My plan to finance this adventure of growing old together was to get back into low voltage wiring at that same company I worked for right out of high school. You know, the one in which I traveled a shit ton and ended up getting charged with a DUI. Well, I still had to travel but not as much as I used to. I had more responsibilities this go around and that included taking care of a company vehicle, going over my jobs for the week and making sure I had the right supplies for each installation. I wasn't just a helper. I was a leader! It felt great to be treated as an adult at such a young age with all those grownup responsibilities I had at the time. Plus, it made me less apt to drink and drive. I didn't want to lose what I had gained. I try not to go backwards if I can avoid it.

That job didn't last long, again, but it wasn't my fault this time. It was a little over a year before the layoffs came. That was a shock to the system. I had bills! I scrambled and was full of fear of the unknown. Was I going to be homeless? Would I have to sell my car? I'm sure I could crash at someone's house for a little bit, but I needed a job. How was I going to live out the dreams my now Wife and I had come up with if I didn't have a stable job?

I searched the newspapers and job boards when eventually I came across another low voltage job. It was a little different than the one I had before. It was all cable TV installations. Boy did I hate that job!

I only kept the cable TV job for 18 months but in those 18 months I put up with a ton of bullshit. Like 12 hour plus days, furious customers, poor working conditions and usually having money taken away from me for the hard work I put in due to some technicality. Bullshit I tell you!

After 9 months of that job, I think I told my boss that I quit every afternoon while turning in all my unused equipment, work orders and invoices for that day. He always told me before I left "See you in the morning Brady!" Sure, as shit, I'd drag my ass in there, slink around and bitch about what I might have to do that day. I wasn't thrilled with the job to say the least. I was back to living in darkness with no end in sight. I was negative and spewing toxicity.

I eventually put in effort to get myself out of that place and found another job. When I put my notice in, my boss was surprised. He couldn't believe that I wouldn't be showing up anymore. I mean, I was one of his top performers even though I did nothing but bitch about my job. None of the day to day crap mattered to me anymore. I could suffer a little longer until my two weeks were over. I was running as fast as I could away from that suck hole and onto greener pastures. I ended up getting back into real low voltage cabling that I used to do but for a new company that mainly serviced local customers.

At the end of the day, the job was a means to an end, and I needed to relieve myself of the stress that was being afflicted on my emotional wellbeing. I told myself that I was heading in the right direction at that point, and I knew I was. I felt like I could sustain this new job long enough for my now Wife and I to start down the road to our dreams.

How far into the future can you see

I'm not going to say that what I decided to do with my career was intended to be long term but deep down I knew I could not pull cable for the rest of my life. Yes, I could do what I did for a couple decades like everyone else, but it was a physically demanding job at times. I remember one job specifically that I was assigned to, where I had been busting my ass all week and decided right then and there that I needed to find something else to do with my career other than manual labor. Every part of my body was in pain, and I was mentally exhausted after each day of work.

I had spent that whole week by myself cabling up a new building for data and voice access to be used by computers and phones. I did most of the work by myself and was tired as shit. Most jobs, I had a helper with me but at that time we were stretched thin around the office, and I was the only one working on the project.

When I was finishing up with the job, a couple of men came on site dressed nice and carrying briefcases. They looked like they had an easy job. Definitely not covered in filth like I usually was from crawling around in ceilings and in tight dusty spaces. Those gentlemen came in and installed some type of hardware that was used to connect all those cables I had ran. At the time, I had no idea what it was, but I knew if I wanted to advance my career, that's what I needed to learn how to do. It felt like a natural progression and possibly my only one.

So, I asked the gentlemen what they were doing, and they replied, "Installing the Network." "What the hell was that" I said to myself. So, after inquiring some more they pointed me into the direction of how I could do what they did. Eventually, I found a college that had a two-year program designed to teach exactly what they did, Networking. It happened to be the same college I attended five plus years ago. The kicker here was that I was working a full-time job. Where would I find the time to go back to college? Well, as usual, there were night classes. If there is a will, there is a way!

I certainly wasn't going to accept that I would be pulling cable into my fifties and knew I had to be the change I wanted to be.

Don't get me wrong, I was okay with what I did at the time, but I wasn't okay with where I was heading. Sometimes in life, you not only have to accept things for how they are but more importantly learn to accept who you are at that point in time. What you do for a living isn't who you are but what you are. What you do for a career is a title and shouldn't define who you are. You can be whatever you want to be in life but learn to accept who you are and what you're capable of, before figuring out whether your career title is part of who you are. Learn to accept who you are today but keep discovering yourself. Who you are now is not who you will be in a few years.

Why accept who you are

You cannot change what you're born with like your hair color, your facial features or whatever. Well, I guess you can change your hair color and facial features nowadays, but my point is to accept that part of you that you see in the mirror and move on.

You still have to accept your human body as something that was given to you. You cannot change your DNA but you sure can work out and eat right to the point that you change your physique. You can most definitely control what you put into your body and how you use it… or don't control it and change your physique in other ways.

Same thing can be said for what you do with your life. If you don't like what you're doing with your life, go out and change it. You have to want it and you have to work for it. Otherwise, it will never happen. Same shit different day, right? That's what I had to do and am still doing to this day. Accepting and moving forward to what I envision for my future. Hence another round of college to course correct the trajectory of my future.

Let's give an example of accepting yourself. Let's say you want to be an astronaut. It's not unachievable but it may not work out for you, right? That's a hard goal to achieve. That's a fact. That's not to say you cannot enjoy space and all the cool science shit that goes along with it. That's called a hobby!

As long as you give it your all, you never know what you'll be able to accomplish. So, what if you don't become an astronaut. What if you just end up being a Rocket Scientist? Would you be ok working within the realms of your dream job in hopes that you may be able to be a part of something bigger? You just might have the chance to be a part of building a vessel to send an astronaut to Space. I think that is way better than becoming an astronaut. Mainly because you get to help someone else live out their dreams that they also worked so hard for but was only able to achieve because of you.

If you're passionate about something but may not be able to be exactly what you want, just be happy with what you have so far in life. Accept that fact and be happy for what you are able to contribute.

At times we will all be faced with the reality of who we are and who we are not. Make peace with it or do something to change it. You can be forgiven of your past as long as you acknowledge it and learn from your mistakes or successes. But the past is just that, the past. Try to look forward to the future and your goals or ambitions. That is who you want to be so go be that. Make the next right decision, right now, in the present, to be who you want to be, in the future.

If the time comes and you feel you've failed at being who you want to be, that's okay. Take what you've learned from those past experiences and keep it with you always. Knowledge is something that no one can take away from you. Once it's known it cannot be unknown.

There are multiple opportunities to learn new things; from either getting to know new people and their past experiences, having to change career paths multiple times in your life, taking the hard road or just going back to college. It's all a learning experience and I was about to find out firsthand what it would take to navigate through it all.

Where do I go from here

While figuring out how to go back to college and determined to not break my back by pulling wire for the rest of my life, I was planning to propose to my now Wife. I was desperately trying to find the right time to propose where she wouldn't see it coming. That was harder than I thought. She was just finishing up her bachelor's degree and we were planning to move in with each other. She expected me to get on one knee at any given moment. Every date we went on, she was anxiously waiting for me to pop the question. And every day that passed and I didn't propose, she got irritated with me. After a while she got so pissed that I hadn't proposed yet, she gave an ultimatum. It was either to propose or say our goodbyes.

What is a man to do in a situation like that? I loved her and didn't want to lose her. The truth of why it took me so long to propose wasn't because I just felt like screwing with her but because the first ring I got was garbage. I couldn't give her a flawed ring. In my superstitious mind that would have meant that our marriage would have been flawed from the start. I scrambled to find a ring that would symbolize the pure love we had. Once I got a better ring than what I initially had, I proposed to her at the first chance I got. That chance happened to be while she was doing my laundry. It wasn't romantic. It wasn't really thought out either. But I will say, she was surprised. I mean who would see it coming when they're folding your underwear?

While we were happily engaged and planning our lives together, we discussed the topic of me finally going back to school to get into Network Engineering so I could get out of pulling wire. We decided that after she graduated in a couple years, and after the wedding, I could go back to college to get a degree in Internetworking. My Wife and I are definitely planners. Nothing got done if we didn't plan for it or set a goal.

I eventually started college and came to realize; I chose a field that required a ton of studying and constant learning. Damnit. I didn't know why I thought it was going to be easy. I really didn't care to put that much effort into getting the degree. I was working hard and didn't want to work any harder to learn something new.

As usual I was falling into a lazy slump of not wanting to change anything and would rather take the easy road, or a handout, but I knew I had to get this done if I wanted to be someone else in the future. I reminded myself that nothing is ever given to you in this life and if you want something you have to go out and get it.

That meant putting in the work and dedicating the time to achieve the impossible. It started to remind me of that time in my senior year of high school when I was facing an uphill battle and had to buckle down to graduate with my class. This time I knew I could rise to the challenge because I had fought that battle before. I had a previous accomplishment to relate this to and give me confidence that I could make it through once again.

Funny thing about this round of college was that I hadn't taken any of my general courses like Algebra and Literature yet. My Literature class was the one that gave me the most trouble. Go figure. I hated writing essays about novels, proper punctuation or using the right grammar. Honestly, I just sucked at it. I was struggling just like I was in high school.

So, I spent a fair amount of time studying in isolation. It took me three full years to finish my two-year degree in Information Technology Internetworking. I had to go all three semesters every year: spring, summer and fall. The main reason it took me so long was because I still had to maintain my full-time job pulling cable. Another reason was because I paid for my own tuition and only had a limited amount of money to spend each semester. On the positive side of paying for your own tuition, I didn't have any school loan debt once I graduated!

I excelled in my studies and really understood what "Networking" was thanks to my background in low voltage cabling. I was happy. I enjoyed what I was learning and found it exciting.

Right before I graduated, I landed a job in the field I was going to college for. I was a Network Operations Center Engineer. Sounds pretty cool, huh? I owe it all to my Wife who gave me the time, opportunity and support to get through college. Without her, I'm not sure where I would be today. She is a blessing that I thank God for all the time. I knew she was good for me back then and that I'd better do anything in my power to keep her around. To this day I'm still trying to "Woo" her to keep her around.

After I graduated and a year into my new career path, I learned that just because I graduated, it didn't mean I was done studying. Yes, I had a degree from an accredited college, but it didn't mean I actually knew what I was doing. Employers in the IT field don't care about degrees as much as I would have thought. They look for experience and certifications that prove you can handle the job. How I saw it was, I had to be certified in certain areas of industry technologies before I was deemed capable and could get a job. The degree was just the beginning. So began my continuing education to earn certifications and man were there a lot of certifications out there to obtain.

So, I studied and studied and studied. My job allowed me to learn on the job and study new networking techniques that advanced my skill set. Which was needed if I ever wanted to move up in the chain of command. My job consisted of twelve-hour shifts for a couple days at a time. During those shifts I had a lot of down time. I was usually alone and didn't have anyone to talk to, so I read and studied all I could without falling asleep at my desk.

The long hours and time to myself was a welcomed gift. I looked forward to the time I could spend reflecting back on what I had learned and what else I needed to learn to keep moving forward. This type of solitude while studying was not intentional but mandatory.

Most of the time when I'm alone, and I enjoy being alone most times, I either read for pleasure or use my time to contemplate areas of my life. I'm an introvert by nature and I find comfort in reading books. I've always been a reader. Ever since the second grade, I had found reading as a way to escape to faraway places. How many second graders can you think of that would choose reading over playing in the dirt or something? Yeah, I thought so. Probably not that many. I'm weird.

Reading was what I enjoyed back then and still to this day I get great joy from learning something out of a book. Most of the books I read were work-related and technical books, but I always found time to balance out my reading with some non-technical books. There has to be a balance. Otherwise, I would get burned out and lose interest.

I would take a break for a few days, or a few weeks, and read some sort of non-fiction self-help book. When I didn't feel like reading, I would go fishing and reflect on what I had learned so far. Stepping away from the books allowed me to put all that I'd learned into perspective. I was able to look at all the information abstractly and then collectively put it together like a puzzle. That method helped in my daily job too. Sometimes I would be faced with a problem at work and had to go for a walk to figure out how to fix it.

Even though I was solidifying my career path by choosing the right certification path and studying my ass off, I still had to stick to the plan my Wife and I created when we decided to get married. All that technical learning was going to lead to a paid day eventually, but I still had to focus on the here and now. We were getting close to a place in life where we could have children, carry on with the day to day, grow old and die. What else could you ask for? Nothing right? Oh right, children.

How do you plan for the unknown

My Wife and I did plan to have children and that time was now! Our plan was to wait until I graduated college before attempting to procreate for a child. It was a great plan and just like a well thought out plan, my Wife got pregnant with our first child within a week or two of trying. Good genetics I suppose?

What an emotional point in my life. Things felt like they were on the right path. We were crushing life goals and creating a family. I felt like I was a full-blown adult.

In the winter of 2012, my son was set to be born. The feeling I felt was mixed around the time of his birth. I was excited to meet the little man but also just hoped everything would go okay during delivery. My Wife and I had spent the last 9 months worrying about him and how he would turn out. My Wife took ultrasound pictures of that baby as much as she could. He was a star before he was even born. The whole term of the pregnancy was going well, and we were to the point where the last thing we had to worry about was the delivery. It was our final scare to get over.

I remember the day my Wife went into labor like it was yesterday. I was working the night shift and just laid down to sleep that morning when I was informed that we had to go to the hospital, immediately. It was time! As all great fathers out there have done before and will do after, I grabbed my racing gloves and loaded the car. I had never been so on point in my driving skills before that day. I should have been a race car driver!

Once we arrived at the hospital the hysteria kind of settled down. We were in the hands of professionals now and there wasn't much we could do but wait for the little guy to arrive. Which took eight hours and my Wife surely appreciated that. Though, when he did decide to finally come out into the world, there was a blast of nervousness in the delivery room. The doctor asked, "Are you ready?" I nodded and thought to myself, "My boy was about to enter this world!" Nothing else mattered to me at that point.

I was in the midst of the miracle of life and was feeling true bliss. That is, until my son was born and wasn't crying. He was purple and still. I locked eyes with my Wife while she turned to look at the doctor in panic and asked, "Why isn't he crying?"

The umbilical cord was tied around his neck and was suffocating him. All the joy I had vanished. Fear set in alongside panic. Thank God for the doctor. She was calm. She controlled the terror of new parents like a champ and carefully handed me a pair of surgical scissors to cut the cord wrapped around my son's neck. I quickly, and with frantic intent, cut that freaking cord with the precision of a surgeon. I wanted my son to live dammit! Once the cord was cut, he was saved but still purple from not having any oxygen. Alarms sounded and the room filled with nurses.

I looked at my Wife and tried to keep her calm even though I was in a state of shock. There was nothing I could do but wait for the doctor and nurses to let us know that our boy was going to make it. Talk about being helpless and hopeful at the same time. After a few gut-wrenching minutes, we were assured he would be just fine. We couldn't hold him just yet and had to wait for hours before we could see him but once we did, I was changed forever.

No longer was I living my life worried about what I would do for my Wife or for myself. No. With the birth of my child I lost all care for myself and only cared about my child. I was no longer able to be selfish for what I wanted. It was all about what he needed. Being a father is the best gift I have received so far in this life, and it wouldn't have been possible if it wasn't for my Wife. I am truly grateful for such a great and powerful woman.

I'll reiterate just in case you haven't followed the chain of events and taken note of how many years had passed but this is my life up until my late twenties. A lot has happened, and I've learned a good bit about life and what being an adult is all about. Don't get me wrong, I was still happy and content with what we had been given in life. I had a good job and a wonderful family now. We lived in a nice house in a nice neighborhood. I was content. There was nothing else that I needed or wanted to do. I was content being a humble servant to my family and sucking up all the wonderfulness of life as a Dad. At least so I thought.

Something was bugging me. Like I had left something undone. I was approaching my thirties and needed a challenge or something to get me through the next 30-40 years of my life. Something to busy myself and my busy mind. I thought if I was distracted enough, I could stay emotionally sound and not lose my shit having a mid-life crisis or whatever the fuck I was going through. Yes, I was constantly studying for new certifications to keep current in my discipline but that became the standard operating procedure of my career. What I needed was a distraction.

I had no idea what else I could take on being a parent of a newborn. I was stretched thin and couldn't take much more time out of the day for anything else. I needed to escape but also couldn't just run from this obstacle. I had to find some air cover so I could maintain the pace of keeping a helpless human alive while working full-time and motivating my Wife enough that she could also keep her sanity. So, one day at work I looked to the future and what I needed to provide for my son so he would grow up to be a great man, and it dawned on me that I was taking for granted me being there to see him when he grew up.

How could I plan for his success if I wasn't taking care of myself well enough to feel like I would still be alive to care for him. What I had been neglecting was my health. I knew I needed to get better at that but all selfishness aside, I did it so my son would have a father when he was older. I was scared I would die early from living like shit. That was the only thing I knew I needed to do at that point in time. I also knew that a workout was enough time to break away from life long enough to recenter my energy and become useful again for my family and at work. I had to start getting serious about my health and exercising. This is when I started to really run and not just run from the police or run from situations in my life. Nope, cardio is what I needed. I was a fat ass and bulking up was not the answer.

Why did I think this was a good solution

Now, I'm not a runner. I absolutely hate running. There's nothing worse in this life than running. Running absolutely fucking sucks. I'd rather lift weights, get on a spin bike, do jumping jacks, burpees, deal with a screaming kid or whatever, except run. It hurt like nothing else. Constantly breathing hard and sweating profusely was not enjoyable. I believe running is the worst thing in the world. I don't like it to say the least but that's not to say that you shouldn't run, or nobody should run. It's just not enjoyable to me, until it's over. Then I wanted more of it. That's what kept me going back out for a run. That runners high! The joy of not thinking about anything else except running.

What I found through running was a way to grow myself emotionally and to analyze or discover how to deal with my emotions and situations better. Working out at the gym helps too, don't get me wrong, but there's something about running that helps me to clear my mind by reflecting back throughout the day to analyze how I had acted emotionally in all my interactions. It was an outlet like none other and I didn't realize how important it would be until later in my life. Running gave me time to think. It became my new alone time. My escape from reality.

The process of running helped me to get over my emotional distress and to get past all the things in my life that were dragging me down. It also cleared my head long enough to find some peace in this whirlwind of a world. You wouldn't think it, but you can go through a lot of emotions just by running.

For instance, some runners experience euphoria while running but some runners experience pain and discouragement. Discouragement in the sense of how hard running is and you should just give up and find some other way to exercise. I seriously have a love-hate relationship with running.

When I started running, I was always discouraged with how far I ran or how I performed but I always got back out there and did better than I had the previous day.

Whatever you go through while running you have to somehow find hope to finish your run without getting discouraged, or to at least get past that mile marker before you walk the rest of the way home. Those are all normal emotions while running. Regardless of what you're feeling, whether before you run or while you're running, you'll feel better once you finish your run. Maybe you'll get past all the thoughts in your head that keep you up at night?

For me, it helped me find peace for thirty minutes at a time when I needed it the most. It was an excuse to get out of the house and find normalcy. That is until my legs started to cramp up one day. At one point it felt like I had torn a ligament in my knee. I wanted to use the excuse that I was born with shitty legs, but I know that's not the right answer. The right perspective is, I probably liked the pain of running a little too much and over did that day. Needless to say, my outlet from life was on hold until I could heal my knee. What was I to do?

In that little amount of time of running, I overcame most of my emotional distress of being a new father with a demanding career. Running gave me the time to go through all of my perceived poor choices. What it also gave me was an avenue to release all the feelings I had bottled up about previous runs or events in my life.

Whatever you may be feeling at the moment or in those past moments that seem to last a lifetime, it takes mental strength to overcome. Mental toughness and awareness of yourself and your thoughts is what can make you a better person and a better contributor to society. You can stabilize your actions through awareness of every emotion or thought, and that will ultimately decide how you should react to any given situation. I can tell you firsthand that running takes a shit ton of mental toughness.

How should I be acting

What I really want to drive home is that everything that has happened thus far in my life was key to knowing who I am now and in this moment in time. For the most part everything I've ever done in my life has been based on what I was thinking at that moment. A lot of it was survival techniques to overcome what I didn't want to be or deal with at the time.

I seemed to only put in effort when I was faced with turning into someone I didn't want to be or doing something I didn't want to do down the road.

Most of my decisions had been strategic with the least amount of emotion. Even those obstacles I faced in high school and college. I wasn't acting out of emotion. I was doing what I had to do to get by. After my son was born, that all changed. I had to be emotional and make decisions that included another human beings' life. I had to make sure that my child would be okay with the outcome of my decisions. I had a feeling within that drove my decisions. That feeling was love. Not your normal love but one that is selfless.

We have all been there. We make life choices based on a deep love for something or someone. Now given, some of those choices may be poor but hey, love is blind sometimes. Although, if you think about it, making life altering choices or critical decisions shouldn't have any emotion included in them at all. They should be well thought out and contemplated thoroughly before acting upon. That may only be possible if you are in tune with your emotions enough to keep them in check and have ample time for response instead of hastily reacting. But that isn't always the case now, is it?

What part of your life can you reflect back on and say with certainty that you made a decision based on love for another human being? How did it turn out? Was it a poor decision or was it the right decision? How did your life turn out because of that event?

I know I've made some piss poor decisions before and most of the time they have not come from love or even for the regard of another individual. I'm sure we all have in some way or another. Take for example a scenario of being angry and frustrated from some event that happened or is happening. Like being fired from your job, someone wrecking into your car or breaking up with a girlfriend/boyfriend because they cheated on you. Then after that event someone walks up to you to ask you a question. Your first reaction may be to sneer at them or brush them off quickly.

I know I've lashed out at people and treated them poorly in those scenarios. It wasn't anything against them or anything. I just didn't care enough to deal with the social aspect of the situation. I was consumed with me and my problems. Not someone else's. You would think they would be more sensitive and give you space right? Well not everyone knows what's going on in our head nor do you know what's going on in theirs. Be considerate in your actions to others and do not include yourself in the situation as being the primary subject of the matter.

Another spin on that same example is, what if instead of being frustrated, you were just depressed or saddened over those same events in your life but it happened from another perspective? Like being demoted, wrecking your car into someone else, or having your girlfriend/boyfriend break up with you unexpectedly? You would probably retract yourself from everything and every event, then go crawl into a little hole and feel sorry for yourself. Oh, it's happened to me more times than I would like to admit and I'm sure you may have felt the same way before. Guess what, your emotional state just hijacked your rational decision-making process.

Here's one last spin on those same previous examples. Think about those times when you were happy? Like when you were on cloud nine and loved everyone but maybe not everybody loved you? Here's the scenario. What if you got promoted, bought a brand-new car or just hooked up with a new girlfriend/boyfriend? Other people may not give two shits about your happiness because they are going through the opposite of your emotional state.

You may not notice it but sometimes people are going through tough situations in their life. They may also do a damn good job of hiding their real emotions. Deep down they may hate you for being happy because they are so depressed or are possibly going through some sort of high priority life crisis that they are jealous of how you are doing compared to them. Do they run a lot?

Be aware of those situations because they could retaliate and make you feel their pain. Always try to lift someone up if you have a feeling they may be in the gutter and not feeling good about themselves. No matter how toxic they may be or how well they think they're hiding their emotions, you have to try to turn them around. Also realize that you are not the only one in the conversation. You actually have to stop talking about how good you have it long enough to figure out how the other person is doing. It's not always about you. If you want friends and want to be a good friend, you have to make other people feel just as important as you would want to feel.

Start a conversation with sincere interest in the other person before you lay your experiences on them. You never know, you might not end up talking about what you intended to discuss. That's what it is really all about. Discovering the conversation that's meant to happen, not the one you want to happen.

You have to be aware enough to not only discover when and what you should talk about but also know to be considerate to other's feelings. Don't talk just to talk or brag about all the things you have or have done but rather make sure what you are saying and doing is respectful to the other person. You may not care about your actions or words but that doesn't mean you're not hurting those that you love and that love you. Remember to be less selfish and consider that your actions could embarrass those who you care about, even if they are not in the discussion. If you care enough about them then consider your own words and actions towards them and other people when they are around. Don't be selfish.

Becoming a father and welcoming my son onto this Earth that we call home, taught me to leave all my selfishness behind and to start to consider someone else's wellbeing before mine. That should be a natural human act but it's not in today's world. Pretty sad realizing that fact as a newfound father and adult. We have the power to change that, but it takes effort and I'm not sure if the majority of the humans on this planet have the capacity to participate. I hope to one day be proven wrong. I'm not sure we have all learned how to be an adult or what all is expected of us as an adult.

Part Two:

Good Times

Chapter 4

Stepping up to the plate

I hate running. I've mentioned that I think but I do consider myself a runner after catching the bug for the short period of running I did before tweaking my knee. For the record my knee was fine. I didn't tear anything per the doctor, but it did give me problems for a couple months. The doctor did mention I had a bone fragment in the back of my left knee. That took me by surprise. I asked if it was a problem and the doctor said, "If your knee starts catching and popping then it could freeze your knee up completely." I thought to myself, "Note taken! I'll be sure to let you know when that event happens." I didn't plan on getting it taken care of right then and there. My theory was that, if it had been in there for who knows how long, that it could stay in there for a bit longer.

I knew I could deal with my knee but what I wasn't prepared for was the realization of how much my emotions were running my life. Since I wasn't actually back to running in the physical sense yet, I was being run by my emotions. I didn't have that time to myself anymore to release all that noise in my head. I was running on pure emotion. Especially with a toddler running around crazy in the house. It was as if my chimp brain was in full effect. I was just bouncing from one kid problem to the next while trying to maintain enough energy to go to work so I could rest.

More often than not we never get a chance to reflect back on our life and analyze how we felt or what we are thinking during certain episodes, and I really needed that in this period of my life. Why did I think I could handle a toddler?

It's hard for us to find the time or solitude to examine our consciousness and understand why we felt the way we did about past experiences and possibly put it all down on paper for review. Why do we get caught up in these emotions that drive our decision-making processes? You would think, being highly intelligent beings, that we could control our reactions in a reasonable and logical way 100 percent of the time instead of acting in haste.

We've been wired to react on emotions since the beginning of time. Before natural language we had to convey our thoughts in the form of external emotional gestures. Just like an infant who cannot speak, we had to express our discontent through kicking and screaming or convey our pleasures through smiling and batting our eyelashes. I'm grateful that we've evolved to the point of being able to communicate with sounds rather than the charade like instances of the past.

In the past couple hundred years we have been able to suppress these primal emotional reactions by the use of mindfulness. Mindfulness is the process of thinking before you speak or "reading the room" before you blurt something out that you'll regret later. It takes awareness of yourself, your surroundings and being present in the moment before you can control your reactions, fully.

Our emotions seem to rationalize all our decisions for us. If you happen to look back and think, "Why did I make that decision?" Is it likely because of how you were feeling at that point in time?

If we try as individuals to overcome our emotions, or at least understand why we feel the way we do, then maybe we can make better decisions in our life and react in a suitable manner in high stress scenarios or day to day activities. The term mindfulness is a way to gain back control of yourself in the world. Just living without thinking or being mindful is not beneficial to you or your perception of yourself.

The goal is to not be controlled by your emotions or have others control you through your emotional reactions but rather regain that sense of confidence in who you are and who you want to be perceived as so you can respond professionally.

How many times have you felt like you were out of control and that you didn't have control over your life? How many times have you been engulfed in some emotion or feeling that was triggered by an action in your life?

We're all guilty of making piss-poor decisions because of how we felt at any given time. We can get caught up in the heat of the moment and that's a natural human function, so don't feel bad. We can all get better at being aware of our emotional states and learn to walk away from situations or react in a civilized manner that may lead to our successes in life.

Just take the example of having a newborn child. If you've ever had a kid, I know you can relate to this one. Not every child is perfect, nor do they all sleep through the night in the first few weeks. Not every child smiles and giggles every hour of the day. Nope. Some babies cry. They cry constantly.

Usually, babies cry for a reason but since they can't tell you why they are crying, it becomes a game of chance. This game can drive you nuts! Talk about being frustrated out of your gourd and on the verge of making piss-poor decisions. A crying baby can make you think irrationally.

Thankfully babies only have a limited number of things to cry about. A few of these are a soiled dipper, they're sleepy and fighting it, they're hungry and need to eat immediately, or my favorite, they need to be burped and puke all over you. I know that's not a complete list but it pretty much sums it up. Being able to keep your emotions in check with a baby as a new parent is a very challenging task. If you can get through that, you can control anything.

Being successful in emotional intelligence and in control of your emotions is key to prosperity. If you cannot control yourself, do you think others will perceive you as a person they want to model themselves after? Even successful people lose their shit from time to time but I'm sure they didn't get to the point of where they're at by being unpredictable, short fused or unreliable.

Have you noticed that successful people always have a success story? It usually starts in their humble past and outlines their struggles and then onto their life changing moments that lead them to success.

Let's get one thing crystal clear. I'm not successful. I do not have a success story. I am not known to all of the world. I'm a guy who has had his struggles and have learned from them.

How do you deal with success

To be successful, you have to define what that means to you. The definition of success may mean different things to different people. To me, being successful is succeeding in my life goals by advancing my career, being able to create business opportunities as they arise and also being the best person I can be in society. Being successful to me is the opposite of maintaining the status quo. You have to move forward to be successful. I am surely not the guy that can stand still long enough to maintain the status quo. I have to be kept busy.

After finding running and getting my career and family started, we moved around a bit and changed jobs a few times. I really can't sit still and most of the time I wasn't thinking things through but rather running purely on emotional reactions to life events. I was just trying to make the best life for my family as I could and took any opportunity that fell into my hands.

The Wife and I made a decision that if our son was to have a decent shot at being successful himself and getting the education he deserved, we needed to move to an area in the country that had excellent school systems and a low rate of crime. In this process of figuring out what we needed to do for the success of our family, I happened to come across a once in a lifetime opportunity. The only problem was that we needed to move across the country, and we only had 30 days to figure out the logistics. Although it was going to be a big change in all of our lives, we faced our fears of the unknown and leapt for the opportunity.

I was being called up into the big leagues. I needed to step up to the plate and face my fears. I didn't have much time to give the opportunity any reasonable amount of thought. I reacted like anyone in that situation and just blindly swung my bat in hopes that it connected with the ball. I was so happy to just be where I was with life and have the opportunity to play the game. This opportunity gave me so much joy. Not only was I finally able to move to a part of the country that I had been in love with for years, but I was moving into a position in my career that had seniority. I was dumb struck with love of life. Love is a driving force that can make you ignorant, as I've mentioned before.

It is only until now while writing this book that I realized why I leapt at that opportunity. I was emotionally attached to the opportunity's location and couldn't see past it to know if I was facing the right direction. For all I knew I could have been standing in the wrong direction in the batter's box, ready to swing towards third base.

Even though I reacted in a tactical approach with my emotions and didn't give myself time to logically think from a strategic perspective about the decision, or it's repercussions, given a second chance I would have made the same decision. It was a once in a lifetime opportunity. It was for the betterment of my family. I had to swing, even if my eyes were closed and I was facing the wrong direction. If you're not playing in the game, you have no opportunity to win.

We moved to Denver, Colorado right before my son turned two. I had a promise of an awesome job for an incredible company. I really respected what they did as a company and believed in their mission. I think that is the most important aspect of a company that you may not realize. It is vital that you agree with what the company does for the sake of your happiness while you work there. Otherwise, you may never be happy and become a crabby person. Oh, it can happen. Believe me!

Although I struggled with the adjustment of a new town and a new role in my career, I wasn't as emotionally wrecked as most. My Wife, for example, did not take the adjustment of the move across the country as well as I anticipated, and I was oblivious to it. I truly was not thinking about what I was doing to her or to her emotional state. I made a tactical decision based on my selfishness and what I wanted. I did believe that this choice would eventually better my family in the long run and knew I had to be the one to make this happen. Selfish or not, it was the best option for my family at the time.

I didn't find out until years after our move to Colorado how detrimental my decision was to my Wife. I found out that she cried for a couple days after the move. I felt like a complete asshole. I had uprooted her from her family and her way of life. She had zero friends and no job. I stripped her of everything. We relied solely on my income and faith that I could maintain employment long enough to stabilize our family in this new town.

I don't regret the decision I made but I do realize that I could have acted with more compassion and empathy in my choice to uproot my family away from our home state. Although if I would have acted from a logical perspective and thought my options through, I don't think we would be as happy as we are today. We would have lived the rest of our lives in Mississippi and not known life anywhere else.

We talk about it to this day and agree, it was the right decision to move. I somehow knocked the ball out of the park on this one and got to round the bases to bask in the glory of accomplishment. It was a great feeling to look back and reaffirm that we had made the right move in our life.

While settling into the move to Colorado and the new job, I hadn't had time to go running. Even though I had healed up from my previous injury and had no reason not to go for a run, I was using an excuse I have told myself time and time again. I was too busy with life. Although I am inclined to give myself a little leeway in this instance. I always tell myself, "There are no excuses but rather only the times when you did or didn't do something. Take responsibility and move forward." But this time I had an excuse. There was the prospect of another child about to come into our family. Yup, baby number two was on the way. What a roller coaster of life so far with one kid but now we have to prepare for a second. I guess things like this are what makes life interesting. It's all about the adventure life brings.

Without running I had to find some other outlet for my peace of mind. I took up hiking and explored a good bit of Colorado. Hiking was easy and it was a family event that brought us closer. I found peace while walking around in the woods. It didn't matter if I struck out by myself or had a baby strapped to my back, I was glad to be in a place without distractions and that had some peace and quiet. Exploring my surroundings, taking in the fresh mountain air and all the unknowns that came with hiking was enough to ease my mind. But then reality knocked on the door. My Wife was pregnant if you recall. She wasn't really into hiking for some reason? Maybe her feet hurt or something. Excuses, excuses, I know!

When does reality come knocking

Even though I had time to go hiking and explore, my job was ramping up too and needed me more than ever. Once again, my peace was short lived, but I was glad for having it for the time I did. I knew I could always get back to hiking at some point but at that time I had to gear up for another child and manage my work life balance better. For over a year, my time was spent with countless overtime hours at work and getting ready for baby number two.

I made numerous decisions within that time based on pure emotions. I didn't care too much about anyone else's feelings but my own. I had no "me" time to recharge. I was constantly on the go, getting shit done. I wasn't perceptive enough to my own emotions, or for that matter anyone else's, enough to know how others around me were feeling. I realized that fact one day and made an effort to slow down so I could be more sympathetic to other's feelings and help them through their troubles.

The truth was, I was being a complete asshole and only taking care of my sanity. My home life was not what it should have been either. I was disconnected from my family and the outside world. Not only was I a mental wreck but I wasn't taking care of my body as well as I should have been. I had stopped working out and lived in front of my computer. I was breaking the promise I made to my son. I felt like I was broken into little pieces and scattered amongst the Earth.

My mind, body and the soul were in ruin. Those elements are the properties of our life that connect us to the rest of the world. If just one of them gets scattered, the rest will lay and waste. I had to repair myself and the only way I could do that was to completely let myself go.

No, I didn't sit on the couch and eat chips while watching television all day. It wasn't that type of letting go. I had to let go of my ego and all that I clung to in life. I stopped caring what I thought of myself and started to care about other people. I opened myself up to do whatever everyone else wanted. I realized I had what I needed right there at home. My family was the most important thing to me, and I wasn't doing them any services by being absent minded to their needs. I hauled them halfway across the country and wasn't being kind enough to do what they wanted to do. I was still taking care of myself. So, I pulled an all stop and started to listen to what they needed.

We should live a life of servitude and inferiority. We are meant to be servants. I'll ask you this, how are we supposed to serve a higher supreme being if we cannot serve each other in which we are nothing more than peers, that are not superior or inferior to one another, but rather judged by experience that are relative to our efforts and time spent meddling?

I believe serving other people first is the only way to be whole again. It brings us all closer together. I can attest, once I started to serve my family, it brought us closer together. Life started to be fun again and I felt like I was falling back into place.

We cannot be whole when we have superiority and power trips for leadership positions. Honestly the best leaders are those that lead by example and serve their people by lifting them up. You will be regarded more for your sacrifice and sufferings than by being demanding and having a controlling demeanor.

The way I see it, I came from nothing. I was gifted this life and it is a blessing. My only service of gratitude I can perform is to go and multiply my talents. To share with the world what I have learned and what I believe to be true. It would be a waste and a disservice to throw away what has so gracefully been given to us all. We all have been given the gift of life. Why would anyone want to squirrel it away for safekeeping like you'll be able to use it in the future? The future is not guaranteed.

After I thought about that perspective for a while, I noticed I had never been sympathetic to anyone, ever. Not only did I need to serve others in my life, but I needed to actually care for them and about them. Odd thought, I know! I wasn't a part of the team. I was trying to win by myself and in today's world, that won't cut it long term. I may be able to hit the ball out of the park sometimes, but I needed the other players on the team to get base hits and even a few homers. At that moment I realized that I needed someone to get an RBI so I could make it back home. So, I cheered my team to victory the best I could.

When you see it, embrace it

I knew I had to change and become a team player if I wanted to grow as a human and move past my faults. Being selfless is one thing I learned from my first child but sympathizing and serving others wasn't going to be easy. I say that because I am a logical person and if you're being dumb, I do not sympathize with that well. Sometimes I set expectations of other people too high. Not everyone can rationalize or has common sense enough to know how to act in public. It's frustrating when things don't meet your expectations. I learned I needed to keep my expectations reasonable to everyone else's capabilities. I needed to change my perception and attitude for the sake of the team.

To change who you are, you have to be able to change attitudes. Starting with yours! It's just like they tell you on an airplane, adjust your emergency oxygen mask before you help others adjust theirs. You have to fix your attitude before you can help others with their attitude. That's how you change. Your attitude is a result of your emotions. If you're negative, then everything and everyone will be shown in a negative light. If you're all tactics, strategy, and run off of getting shit done all day without real regard for your fellow man, then what type of person do you think that would be? A hard ass.

I think that kind of attitude change for more compassion and empathy towards others should be a mandatory kind of game changing life achievement that needs to be taught at a young age and not learned in your thirties. Once you realize you need to change, don't give in and give up on your faults but rather acknowledge your weakness and be mindful of them so you can overcome them one shit quality at a time. I realized I've missed out on a lot of opportunities to get to know people better by not being more attuned to others' state of emotion they were in at that time. I disregarded their emotions and only wanted to convey what I wanted them to feel. I was important, right?!

I noticed this even more when my second child came into this world. The experience that came with the second child was way different than the first. I was preparing for the end of the world with baby number two.

Leading up to the day my second child was born was less stressful than the first to say the least. The Wife and I knew what to expect this go around and somehow chilled out when we got closer to delivery day. We packed our bags with a couple days of clothes and a few of our favorite snacks. We made sure we had the car seat installed in the car along with all the rattles and shiny stuff for the kid to gaze at. It also helped that we had an appointment schedule for delivery. Talk about taking out all the excitement.

On the day of delivery, we loaded up in the vehicle and casually drove to the hospital. As we arrived at the hospital, I passed by the emergency entrance and went down to the long-term parking where I pulled into a spot near the back. It felt like it was just an average day. No rush. No panic. We were all smiles.

Once we got into the hospital and checked into our room like we were on vacation at some resort, the nervousness sat in. There was nothing else to do but to wait for the nurse to come in and start to induce labor.

Even the process of the nurses getting my Wife ready for delivery was laid back and unrushed. It wasn't even an hour after we had arrived, checked into the room and got the Wife strapped in, when the doctor stepped into the room. The doctor introduced herself and examined my Wife. After her assessment she noticed the baby was already coming out! The nurses quickly shifted my Wife into position and a half a push later my child was born. The Wife and I looked up at each other and were stunned at how quick and easy this delivery was compared to our first born. Then we gazed at the doctor while she wrapped up the child and handed it to my Wife.

It was a girl. Oh my, was I in love. Not like I wasn't in love with my first child when he was born but a father-daughter bond is different from a father-son bond. I'm grateful to have had a healthy son and daughter. I know most people are not that fortunate and we all pray for the health of our children. Not only when they are born but throughout our entire lives.

With my daughter coming into this world, I found a different kind of love. It was that empathetic kind of love I had been searching for and needed. I felt what she was feeling and was compelled to do all I could to make her happy. If she was distraught or not pleased in any way, I had to make it right. This life changing event ultimately changed my perspective of others in my life and I started to serve people with true intent to make them happy. To this day I realized that I may have felt empathetic for other people but not in a manner that I would do something about it. That thought scared me. How many other people have the same outlook? Think about that.

Would you help someone you didn't know or even kind of knew out of empathy for them? Probably not. We just don't care. We are too caught up in our own lives to inquire into someone else's. Sometimes we even disregard the lives of those closest to us like our friends and family. We get spun up in the tornado of our life and don't care about anything else. When in actuality, our life should be full of everyone else's life and making sure they are okay. When was the last time you started a conversation wanting to know how someone else was doing and didn't have the inclination to discuss what was going on in your life? How many times did you say the word "I"? We like to show people how important we are to them right? We are important to a degree, but not as important as other people. You need them more than they need you.

I learned from my daughter that I should consider not only my feelings and emotional state but be cognizant of others I interact with and their current state of mind. I believe I truly started being a father and a husband after my daughter was born. I know that's probably horrible to say but it's true. I think it's sad that it took me so long to realize that I wasn't important anymore. I had to step up to the plate and start playing the game in hopes that I can help lead my fellow teammates to victory.

Chapter 5

Something to believe in

With everything seemingly going good in my life after a massive amount of change for my family and career, there was something bound to not sit right at some point. That something was me. I got bored! I wasn't running. I wasn't getting outside much. I wasn't advancing my career fast enough. I couldn't sit still, as usual. I had to meddle and muck with my life just to keep myself entertained and distracted from all that was going on at the time. At least, that's what I told myself.

So, I did what any emotionally rational human being would do. I started looking for another job that would take my career to new heights. It's not that I didn't like my job or who I worked for, but I wasn't progressing to where I thought I should have been in my career for the few years I was there. First thing I did with my uncomfortable feeling was run the idea of a job change by the Wife. She agreed that it was an okay decision but had one ultimatum. We would not be moving! I agreed. I knew that if I was going to change something in my life that I needed to check with my loved ones and get their opinion first. Not that I'm driven by their influence but because I wanted to make sure they felt okay with what I needed to do. I learned from my past, that I wasn't in sync with my loved one's feelings and needed to make decisions that did not reflect poorly on their emotional state. Especially my Wife and kid's feelings. Again, if you're not learning, you're not moving forward. I had learned from my previous shortcomings, of my disregard for someone's feelings towards my decision about moving across the country, and knew I had to involve them in my thought process before I acted up on them. I had to be a team player if I wanted my family to stay together.

As I began down the road of job hunting and into the interview circus, I was hopeful. Hopeful that I would land somewhere where I would be respected and regarded as an equal, or better yet a leader. Something I was not getting at the time. I sought out leadership roles. I had enough certifications and experience in my field of studies to land a great position at a large company. Again, I was hopeful and that was not the state of mind I should have been in.

Hope is an emotion that we gather from our feelings about a certain object or situations. It is a very powerful emotion that some people rely on every day. There are many different use cases that people apply hope in. Hope is that emotion that fills you with complete joy on the "what ifs". In my opinion, it's abused by most people and can lead to pure ignorance out there.

As a culture we argue the what-ifs instead of focusing on what will or had actually happened. What if, should not be how we judge someone either. We should judge them on what they did, not on what they would have done, if.....

We want to justify our morals and beliefs by the what-if because we disagree with someone else's actions or beliefs. What if you were the person that was being judged by your actions and beliefs? That feeling of being judged can be unsettling. Why would you want to make someone else feel that same way? You should be questioning your actions in certain situations and what it would do to your integrity or the integrity of others. Don't question somebody else's actions and motives unless you can actually put yourself in their shoes. The hope is, you can see both sides of the argument.

Who did what

In an argument there is usually the accuser and the accused. For the most part the accuser is the one who has an issue. The accused is the one to be damned. We are all out to condemn the accused. Regardless of if we know the back story or not, we always side with the accuser for some reason but never seem to put ourselves in the situation of the accused, or for the sake of argument, the accuser. To be honest, half the time the accuser is out to better themselves and feels like they have been treated unfairly, so they throw a fit towards the accused. But in our society, we're blinded by that because we are so caught up in our what-ifs and don't actually see the truth or motives behind the accuser or even the accused. Our role in these accused versus accuser situations for the most part are outside hecklers. We are fueled by instigating and voicing our opinion in a matter that usually doesn't even affect us. Why do we act like this? Do we need attention?

Some accusers like to lay everything on the line in hopes that they will get something in return. As to believe that if they apply all their energy into their hopes that they will receive all kinds of glory. This is hardly logical thinking. It's an emotional state. Hope is an emotional state. You have to create more than a theory to come to a conclusion. You cannot just hope for something and expect to get it. That's fairytale thinking. Take our political system for instance. Have you watched the actions and gestures of our government representatives? They seem delusional and they act out of spite for one another. Maybe it's because they've spent too much time in the circus? I certainly believe that too much time doing one particular job can make us blind to the day to day operations and derail us from the real matters at hand.

I feel as though our government is rigged and there is no hope in course correcting it. It feels like no one is there to help us. They are there to help themselves. They accuse each other of petty injustices and act like school yard children. We watch the made for TV reality show of our government with the same outside heckler role as we do for everything else. We side with whoever screams and kicks the loudest without actually understanding the reasoning behind the outburst.

Serving our country in a position of power should be a privilege. It should be something you are chosen to do for a reasonable amount of time. I also don't believe you should be voted in by our also seemingly rigged election system. I feel as though you should be drafted.
What if all our representatives were drafted into position and had a 6 year term to serve our country? Now keep an open mind here, it could work. The first year could be used to learn from the existing person in position. The next four to lead and the last one used to transition out by teaching the next in line. Also, what if there was basic government housing for those and their families. You know, barracks. There could also be a stipulation that their previous employers had to honor their employment on their return of service just like we do for our military.

One last idea, while in service to our county and on departure, you get to make a minimum wage salary. I'm hopeful that this what-if could come to fruition. Anything is possible if the masses can agree on it. Wink!

When hope is all you have

Hope is a fickle feeling though. It comes and it goes. Just like watching political debates, it includes the range of emotions like happiness, joy, sadness and fear. These emotions can swing from one spectrum to the other and engulf your whole being. Hope is one that we cling to in our times of suffering, in our times of joy, in our times of regret and in our times of deceitfulness. We cling to hope. Hope allows us to change our feelings from one to another. Hope can be very dangerous if we allow it to take over our rational brain. We may end up hoping all the time. Like hoping those in government positions would be thrown out to the curb to be tarred and feathered because we're butt hurt and disagree with their perception of the world.

There are times when I can say that hope has led me down the wrong path. Hope has guided me in the wrong direction many times. One time I hoped I had this certain type of vehicle because I was into off-roading and I thought that if I could own it, that I would be able to do all this great outdoors and adventurous stuff. I was wrong. It turned out to be a money pit. I could have spent that money on a different vehicle and got the same results for less money. That's not an extreme example but you get the gist.

Sometimes we need that misdirection, so we can go down that path to learn what not to do in the future. I've been down some paths that were very hard and dark too, but as I look back, I am glad I had hope to misguide me so I could learn the truth about my misconceptions.

Hope isn't all bad though. Sometimes good can come from it and lead you down a more grateful path. For instance, I had hoped that one day my father could be a better man and I could be more involved with him. That day came, and I'm much happier after I was able to clear the air with that man.

When I was younger, I had hoped that one day I would find a beautiful woman that I could call my Wife. That day came as well, and I couldn't be any happier.

What are some of the moments in your life where you relied on hope to answer your problems? Did it work out? Did you learn anything from it? Did you get what you wanted or what you needed?

Some call hope, faith and say that we have to have faith to survive. If you're constantly finding yourself in dramatic situations where you grasp at hope in the midst of desperation and find some form of relief that digs you out of whatever hole you have created for your life, then maybe you need to change your perspective. Somehow, we tell ourselves that if we have faith, and if we believe strong enough, that we will persevere. That everything will work out. Well, that's all the kinds of bullshit that you read in fairy tales about princesses and unicorns. Be real and quit lying to yourself. Wake up and know that you are not helpless and can make a change for the betterment of yourself and others. You just have to put in real effort. Hope alone will not make change. You have to take action to change the things you hope for. Hope alone is just wishing.

The real-world crushes hope. It crushes faith. Life will crush your hopes and dreams. Hope sucks ass!

Hope seems to take control of all of your emotions. It takes control of your joyfulness, your sadness and your anger. What I mean by that is, that hope can take your sadness and turn it into happiness. It can also take your happiness and turn it into fearfulness or sadness. Hope can also make you angry if you sit around hoping someone will act on something you want to happen, but they never do. Hope will drive you nuts if you let it.

What do you really need

I've learned that the only way to control the emotion of hope is to let things in your life go. You have to let things be. Same can be said for our current state of politics. I'm hopeful we can implement a system that is fair to all and not beneficial to only those who have an exuberant amount of money. But I know that is something that I shouldn't be focused on every day. I'm hopeful but not obsessed and reliant on how much hope I put into my wants. I'm not going to get angry if nothing ever happens. I will accept it and move forward.

You can't let things take control of you like hope. If you're fantasizing that what you want is really what you need, you need to either put in the work for what you actually need or stop wanting so much. We have to let go of our materialistic lives and quit having so much hope that if we obtain something that it will make us happy or make us better. Like new politicians.

When you strip all your materialistic possessions away, you're left with only one thing, time. The most precious gift on this Earth. It's the one that most of us take for granted and shouldn't be spent hoping for change. Prisoners, for instance, claim to have nothing but time. They have nowhere to be and nowhere to go. Their life has been stripped away down to the only thing most of us humans neglect to appreciate. Time.

We are too busy trying to be important. As if we are somebody of importance! No matter how important being important may be in your world, you have to learn to leave that shit at the door. Nobody wants to hear how important you are. They want to hear how important they are! At the end of the day, it's a popularity contest of who is the most popular person in town. Why would you want that?

We should strive to be nobody. What if you had everything stripped from you? Your identity was wiped away. No bank accounts. No home. No car. No family. No name. Nothing. Even the memory of you had been wiped from your family and friends' minds. You meant nothing to anyone and had nothing. Would you be ok with that? Would you still be able to wander this Earth?

I bet you wouldn't! It's an uncomfortable thought, being unimportant. But if you're ok with it and realize you were never anything important to begin with and are just lucky to be alive, then you may start to live a happier life. You were not important to anyone other than your parents when you were born. And after you die, you may still not be important to anyone. Be okay with that.

If somehow you do go down in the history books and become someone who "was" important some time ago, great! You'll be dead, and it won't matter much to you then so why should you care about being important while you're alive.

Don't get me wrong. You can be important while you're alive but do it for the right reasons. Be an important servant. Treat others like they are your superiors. Because if you want to feel important, you have to treat others as if they are just as important as you, if not more than you.

It doesn't mean that we should lose faith or hope altogether because nothing should ever matter to us anymore. No. As with anything, there is a balance. You have to balance your wants from your needs and your hopes from your realities. Do not get caught up in wishing for your wants but rather take what is given to you as you need it. Otherwise, you may become delusional and chase after things that have no potential or won't matter in the end. Like political bickering. Get to work!

How high are your expectations

The thing about hope is that it has the potential to leave you distraught and torn up inside if you rely on it too much. I once saw my kid after a baseball tryout ceremony where he was so eaten up inside because he didn't win any part of the competition. It just killed me to watch him go through this. By the way, he is just as emotional as I was when I was a young boy. I should have expected this, but I was hopeful he would take after his mother. Who is a rock!

He had hoped that he would win one of the three competitions of either running, batting, or throwing. He thought he was the best kid out there. His expectations were high, but he didn't know that. He's just a kid. Let me tell you though, this kid is a pretty fast runner but when it came down to the awards at the end of a three-hour tryout in 90-degree heat, my son broke down once the awards were announced. He didn't finish in first place, nor did he finish in the top three. He got nothing for his efforts. He bawled his eyes out for an hour. He had lost all of his hope in the world and faith in himself.

All of his hopes and dreams were gone. He was so crushed he did not want to do anything. His whole world was flipped upside down. All I wished for, was for him to just let it go and stop worrying about him not meeting his expectations. This is just a five-year-old boy, imagine what happens as an adult when we keep the same fairy tale mentality that hope instills in all of us.

I know it may be a little extreme and distorted but as adults we still do the same thing in our everyday lives. We use hope to instill some sort of happiness in our lives, that if we obtain this or that, that we will be good to go. I bet you've seen or heard people so enraged in anger over something not working out for them that they had hoped someone would just die so they could get their way. It's sad but true! Some people have a distorted view of their world and sometimes they obtain the mentality of a stubborn child. Maybe they never let it go? Maybe they will never grow up? We totally think that we are going to get what we want! Just like a five-year-old.

Another example of dealing with hope is that I may play the lottery from time to time and hope that I'm going to win the jackpot but when my expectations aren't met the next day when I don't have the winning lottery ticket, I don't shut down and lock myself in a dark room and stay there for a month wallowing around all torn up inside with disappointment. No! I know what the expectation is. I know what the outcome is going to be. I don't put all of my faith into what I am hopeful for. That's the deal. Set your expectations low and take what comes to you. It will relieve you of so much burden of not getting what you had hoped for just by lowering your expectations a little bit.

If you spend all your time hoping for things in your life, you'll never understand the things in your life that you already have that you should be grateful for. One thing that I've learned from hope is that I already have what I need, and anything extra, is a bonus. I have already won the lottery! Not literally, but I feel lucky in life. I have a wonderful family. We live in a nice middle-class home. We don't have much debt. Life is good!

From now on I live my life hopeless. Hopelessly in love with all the things that I never wanted or ever thought I could ever have or achieve in my life. Today I am truly happier. One emotion I love to keep around is gratitude for what I never knew I needed.

That's not to say I don't catch myself being hopeful anymore, because I do. I just don't have high expectations of anything as often as I might. Things will happen or they won't, regardless of how much effort you put into something. Sometimes good will come and sometimes bad may be the result of it, but as long as you can discern the reason as to why things happened later down the road, you can live a life of understanding and rationality.

When it comes to knowing if something is going to work out for the good or bad, you may have a tough time figuring that out. I was about to go through that process firsthand. If you don't recall at the beginning of this chapter, I started to look for a job. During my job search I stumbled upon that leadership role I was seeking out. It seemed like a dream job. It had the title that I wanted to have in my career, but it also had the responsibility to prove to myself that I was worthy of such a role. I lucked up and got the position. I was filled with joy and happiness. My level of hope and expectations were high!

I started the job and started taking in so much information, that it was like I was drinking from a fire house. It was a fast-paced environment with high energy. Looking back, I truly enjoyed that pace. At least for a few months I enjoyed it. When the pace didn't slow and the stress started to pile on, my hope started to diminish. I was beginning to become something I did not like.

Part Three:

Bad Luck

Chapter 6

It happens

Alright... Alright....

It was alright. For a while. While navigating life at the new job and enjoying the pace of being a busy leader, I started to realize I wasn't as respected as I thought I would have been. I was still viewed as a young and inexperienced individual. Someone who had no say so and was viewed as being inferior and lacking any and all kinds of intelligence.

At least that's how I felt. It may not have been the actual case, but I was so caught up in my work and other aspects of my life that I had no time to think rationally. I was making all my decisions based on the emotion I was in, at that moment in time. And let me tell you, I was an emotional wreck, again. I could take being an inferior or being a servant but when you get stepped on, time and time again, you will eventually tell yourself you've had enough.

There seemed to be a pattern emerging. Stress and insignificance were equaling an emotional response from me. I became rationally blind. Everything I had learned from my past was wiped clean. I was a regular knuckle dragging ape going through the motions.

As days went on, I spent the majority of my time fighting fires at work by solving problems and resolving technical issues. What I was doing was useful to others and it seemed like I was making progress. Which left me with a sense of accomplishment from what I was completing at work. Other times, I was sad and disappointed over my decisions. This feeling was increased even more so from the responses of my peers and superiors which were negative and always ruthless. I felt like a failed leader.

As a leader of my family, I knew I had felt this feeling before. I tried to encourage myself that it was only temporary, and I could endure through but at the end of the day, I was stuck with disappointment.

Why am I so angry

The majority of my time spent in that position and at that company, I was someone I didn't enjoy. I was becoming an angry and spiteful person. I was angry at everyone and everything. Mainly because of all the situations I had been put in but regardless of it all, I was becoming a bitter and toxic person. I was full of hate which led me to become angry at the world.

Out of all the emotions, there should be no room for hate. I say "should be" because all the rest of the emotions are natural. Hate on the other hand is bred. You have to be taught to hate something. You have to be coached into disliking something often enough that you begin to have a different feeling about it. Something so definite that you can feel it in your bones. You hate it! It's brought on by persistent negativity and it can overwhelm the most positive among us all. Once you're full of hate, the only emotion you can muster up is anger.

Anger can be stemmed from fear, or even sadness depending on the situation. In my case it was both. I was sad that I had gotten myself into that situation and fearful of what it would take to get out of it.

Hate seems to build within us into some sort of fury or compulsive rage. This fury is a negative energy towards some balled-up resentment within our belief system. Anger fueled by hate can cause us to do the most irrational actions and gestures just like love, but unlike love, it benefits us rather than the receiver. Anger can give us a type of satisfaction that seems to only help us when we act from its emotion.

Our actions from anger will never help anyone on the receiving end. It will only hurt them. We may spit out verbal attacks and expressions from our anger that we will surely regret later. I'm at fault for being angry at this point in my life. Anger out of disbelief of what was going on around me, but more importantly, I was angry from the realization of the fakeness in the everyday social interactions. Think about the minutes that you could have back from being angry. You are wasting your time!

There is so much anger deep within us, as well as in our hearts, against people in our lives. So much so that we become someone who is not genuine and not who we really are at times. Our sincerity is visibly washed away when dealing with these people. We become blind to everyone else's emotions and feelings. We don't care what the results are as long as we get some sort of satisfaction from our actions. Most of the time we want sweet revenge when we are angry.

When you get mad at someone, what do you do with the perception of them? We tend to lock them up in that little jail cell in our brain and will not let them free because of anger towards them in a way that condemns and modifies our perception of them. We change our perception of who they are to the point that we are disgusted with them or resent them so much that it makes us furious to even think of them. There is no convincing us that they should be let free from that jail cell for what they have done to us in the past.

Whether it's from a disagreement or for their beliefs in some aspect of some given situation, we tend to hold them accountable for being different from ourselves.

We can be stubborn and disregard them as actual human beings when angered to the point where we wish they would be better off dead or to never have known them in the first place. We lock them up in our mind's jail. That's a hard place to get out of especially if you happen to be the one locked up in someone else's jail. Be careful when that happens. I've been there, and in a time when I was already angry at that person, which made me even more furious.

More times than not, I get angry out of my sadness for other human beings on this planet. My anger comes from what I cannot do for my fellow man. My anger comes from my fear that if I can't do anything to prevent an action from coming into fruition that it might materialize into something negative for all individuals involved. I have a tendency to try to stop all the bad things from happening, and if I can't, I get mad. I feel like a superhero. I know I cannot change everything bad in this world, but I sure do like to try as if I can. Sometimes I get to the brink of tears when there is a situation arising that I see is going to turn out bad, and I know there is nothing I can do about it. I do recognize that having compassion for other's well-being should be a normal reaction, but I feel it in a deeper sense of responsibility. I truly care.

I'm not sure you can relate but I'm sure you can understand and rationalize what you've just read. That anger is not brought about on its own. It is derived from other severe negative emotions that we feel in our everyday lives. Listen to your emotions and hear what they are saying to you.

What I would like to see is a resolution of fear in people's hearts. A resolution of disheartened people in this world. The only way to obtain that and to control our anger is to control your reaction to others and the situations you may be in. Also, don't fear other people and what they might do, even if it's tied to their beliefs.

Take a look at all the news on TV and in the papers today. It can be an information overload, for sure. A lot of that information can leave you in a panic when it's made out to be a bigger deal than it should be. Learn to not let it bother you and don't take it personally. Easier said than done I know. Sometimes it is anxiety provoking and can lead to taking medication that we don't need to be on long-term. Ugh...

Why take prescription drugs? If you have to take them forever, are they really doing you any good? Do they help you or make your illness worse? Do they keep you feeling like you did before you took them? Don't let them be your crutch in life. At the end of the day they are your excuse for why you're not good enough.

That's not to say some people out there don't need medication because we all know some people truly need it. But my point is, don't rely on it to save you. You have to help save yourself too. The medicine should only help you along the way to recovery and not be something permanent.

Why are you anxious? What is frightening you to the point of a panic attack? Your past experiences? Yes! That is exactly why we get anxious and freak out in certain situations. It's because something has happened in the past in a similar situation that turned out bad.

Instead of being scared of the "What-if it happens again?" or "What am I going to do next time?", you should be confident. Confidence that you made it through the past instance and this instance should be no different. You made it past that previous instance and eventually, this instance will be in the past as well.

What about when you read or hear about a horrific story in the news? You may feel sadness and want to intervene into other people's lives to help or save them in a way, right? Sometimes that sadness can put you on the verge of anger because you feel helpless that you cannot take action in the matter. That's okay. We are one in the same. That's normal. But don't let it overtake your rational mind and lead you into depression where you feel as though the only way out is through drugs. The only way to solve any of that is to get out there and help people, one by one and face to face. Get over your fears of helplessness and have sympathy for other people in this world. Your feelings have a superhuman power to them. You can change your feelings without the use of drugs. Learn to listen to them and not be controlled by them.

You can't be happy all the time!

My hate may never go away. I have this fuel cell of hate buried within me. It doesn't seem to ever get depleted, but I feel as though it grows. I only say that because once I feel disappointment, I tend to get angry and this hate for any and all opposition boils up. Once that happens, the fire within me burns for a long period of time. I smolder.

It took some time to reflect back on this aspect of myself while trying to maintain my sanity at that frantic job and I began to realize that I was getting angry for no reason. A lot of those instances were out of my control. I was angry because of my misfortune and not because someone intentionally meant to do me harm.

Then I asked myself, "What kind of idiot am I?", and felt sorry for all those people that stepped in the way of my fury of hate. My anger may be buried inside me for the rest of my days on this Earth because this world is so messed up, but hey, that's another reason why I go running. Was I running though? No. It didn't even cross my mind that I should be trying to alleviate my frustrations. I was too caught up in the hate sucker punch I gave myself.

With all the crap scenarios and situations going on at that job and in my personal life, it took a minute to see through all the anger and other emotions I was dealing with. I eventually broke out of the feverish fury and asked myself "What the fuck am I doing?" Seriously! I had lost all touch with what I was trying to accomplish. My goals were lost. I didn't have a plan. I wasn't a good father or husband. Again. I felt lost. I ate like shit too.

Heck, I didn't have much time to do anything but stress and be an asshole. I was so consumed with everything going on in my life that I was neglecting my promise to my son, to be a healthy person and to be there for him and my family. Being stressed out and pissed off all the time is not very healthy.

So, I struck out running one day. At first, I was only able to run three quarters of a mile before I was sucking wind, but eventually after a few days I got up to finishing three mile runs. I really only ever planned to run two miles every time I ran, and then end up walking over a mile back with some sprints in there. It was difficult and I have no idea why I thought it was a good decision to start running again. I knew I needed to exercise and was tired of lifting weights all the time, but I needed a distraction from the real world for whatever short amount of free time I had, so running was my answer.

I realized I didn't feel anything after my first couple of runs, except for the pain and suffering of not running in a long time. What was more intriguing to me was that I wasn't angry afterwards. I was numb. I had forgotten what I was pissed about during my run, but more importantly, I was calmer than I was before I started running. I guess I was as calm as you could be after running a couple miles but nevertheless, I wasn't focused on work. I was more focused on my legs cramping and if I'd be able to even walk the next day.

I did those runs for a few months until I felt comfortable and then upped it to four miles each time, and then six miles. Those six milers would be my long runs I would do on the weekends when I had more time.

You never know when you may be walking for a few miles, so I planned to give myself extra time to get the miles in regardless of if I was running or walking the last couple miles.

I ran more frequently after that and the pain that came with running was less frequent as well. The more I ran and focused on my next run or what route I was going to take, the more I disconnected from all the shit going on in my life. I was focused on running and not paying attention to anything else in my life. I had fully escaped my reality. Screw all the noise at work. All I cared about was running.

At one point I even got the opportunity to run in a real race. My first ever race! I was excited to compete and do something I had never done before. It was a 7k around downtown Denver which meant it wasn't too long and that I could definitely finish it. I trained for a few weeks leading up to the race, running three miles every other day.

When it came to race day I was pumped. I ended up running sub eight minute miles which was fast for me.

There's something about running in a race that keeps your pace up higher than if you were to run alone. I'd have to say it's the competitiveness of the race that kept me running faster and longer than I normally would have.

Now my sub eight-minute mile pace didn't warrant me winning the race or anything. Oh no. I placed somewhere in the middle. That was fine with me. I was just glad that I could compete and that I wasn't as angry or emotional as I had been in the past few months. I was really just happy to be doing something else with my free time other than working.

How long will it last

After that race, I kept the running routine going. It seemed to help me mentally. It was like a hobby. I got past all the bullshit going on in my life by exerting myself for thirty minutes to an hour at a time. On top of running, I was also lifting weights. I felt like a beast. I was doing more physically than I ever thought I was capable of doing. My mentality had changed. My perception of myself was morphed into a sense that I could accomplish anything and tackle any situation. Well, there is some truth to that but as the saying goes, "nothing lasts forever".

A few months after that race, I was running longer distances. My wonderful Wife had also taken up running. She would usually only go running in the mornings when I wasn't running. The majority of the time she would go with her neighborhood friends. They like to run races too. 5k's, 10k's 15k's and eventually half marathons.

Sometimes when we had someone to watch our kids, we would run together. One day we went running together because she was training for a 15k. She wanted to get a long run in a couple weeks before her race, and we found a time to go run in the Colorado countryside. It was a 10 miler through western Colorado farmland. It was a beautiful run, and it was also the furthest I had ever attempted to run.

Seeing as I had never run that distance before, I was running at a much slower pace of 11 to 12 minute miles. I didn't want to overdo it. I'm pretty good at putting in more effort than my body can take. At least that's the excuse I tell myself when I get injured and wouldn't you know it, my knee was jacked up not even two days after going on that long run with my Wife. The only thing I wish I would have done differently after that run, was to stretch. I should have stretched for an hour or so after that run but I didn't. I was stiff and neglected what my legs were telling me. So, I had to quit running, again.

A few days after that run, my knee seemed to get worse. It was brutal. I had done something to my knee that made it unbearable to run, walk, sit or just get out of bed. I went and saw a doctor. I thought that maybe that bone fragment may have gotten lodged somewhere it shouldn't have been. A doctor warned me that this could happen. Maybe this was that time?

Once I was examined by a physician and the reports came back, they were baffled. They said it wasn't a tear and it wasn't the bone fragment either. That was still in the same place that it's been for who knows how long. They said they needed to do an MRI to figure out what the issue was. Wellbeing a stubborn man, I decided to go my own route. Mainly because I didn't want that doctor bill for an MRI and all the other tests they would have done just so they could tell me there was nothing they could do. So, I suffered through the pain for six months. At times I tried running when I thought I was healed up, but my knee would cramp up and start hurting only after a half mile into my run. Let me tell you that half mile walk back home was not enjoyable.

I knew that I would have to take another break from running. I did some research online like all paranoid people do when they are sick or feeling some sort of discomfort and I found an article that seemed to outline my exact symptoms. I thought I had suffered an iliotibial (IT) band injury. It all seemed to line up with what I was feeling. The only way to get past it was to stretch and give it time.

I still wanted an outlet for my life so I could cool the smoldering of my anger and since I couldn't run, I started lifting weights more often. I even got a spin bike. I healed up after six more months of stretching and not running or doing any form of weighted leg exercises. For those of you not doing the math, that was a year of not being able to run after initially injuring my knee after the long run with my Wife.

For some reason the spin bike I had was the only thing that seemed to not irritate me. I didn't understand it at the time, but I was taking what was given to me. I could sit on that bike for hours and slip away from all my troubles while the hate soaked sweat poured out of my body. It was a great substitute but nothing like going for a run.

When it happens, stop and think

After getting past my injury and still trying to relieve myself of all the negativity of my life by working out harder and harder, I eventually decided to leave that job I had, and the feeling was mutual. It hurt me mentally. What hurt me the most was that they wanted me to leave more than I wanted to leave. So, I separated from the company and was left without a job.

Regardless of the situation at that time, I was already in the process of my exit strategy anyways and wanted to leave all that negativity behind. Although now I had to work harder to find another opportunity for employment. I needed revenue coming in so I could take care of my family.

I will say, it hurt deep down to know that I wasn't wanted at that company. Especially after all the work I had put into every aspect of my day to day tasks. I truly cared about what I was doing and why I was doing it.

I lost all faith in my abilities, self-esteem, and questioned who I was after I left that company. I had some time after separating myself from that job to collect myself and look internally to understand who I was and what the hell I was doing with my life.

Was I good enough? Did I actually have the abilities that I thought I had? All this questioning started to cast doubt in my mind and fuck with my self-esteem.

I ended up finding a new job two month later and had some time to reflect on what I had just been through. I realized I still wasn't back to the confidence level I was before I left my last position. I was so depressed, I considered blowing my brains out. At one point I grabbed my gun out of my dresser with the thought of doing myself harm. I looked up and saw a picture of my kids on my dresser and felt like an idiot. I immediately separated my gun and the bullets it had in it. I guess this was to make it harder for me to perform the act if I was feeling this way again? I didn't think it would help much but at least there was some resistance.

What really got me through that tough time and not acting on my emotionally driven plan was the constant thought of imagining my kids without their father. Even though I did nothing but scream at them and felt like a complete waste of life, I still couldn't go forward with suicide because of the empathy I had toward my Wife and kids. I couldn't imagine how they would feel if I had gone through with it.

Have you or someone you know, had a close friend or loved one commit suicide? How did you feel? I did not want that weight on my family's shoulders.

I felt like the scum of the earth and wanted to die. I showed it well too. I yearned for everything to stop. I didn't want to continue. My emotions were taking control and almost led me to the point of no return. I would have ruined the lives of my family if I would have acted rashly from my emotions. Knowing and understanding what I meant to others ultimately saved me from the wreck I had become. I will note that I **didn't** reach out and talk to anyone about what was going on in my head. I just walked around slowly with my head down and had a sad look on my face. Not once did anyone actually inquire to see if I was truly okay. I had a few people reach out to help me find another job, which was wonderful, but no one asked how I was doing mentally. Maybe I'm perceived to be tougher than I felt?

Once I was able to rationalize like a normal human being again, I was able to start to formalize a plan to get my life back on track. That plan was to continue to provide for my family and prove to myself that I was as good as I knew I was. I also had to prove that I wasn't the asshole I made myself out to be. I had put myself in my own mind's jail cell. I had changed the perception of myself to be so negative that I didn't want to hear shit I had to say. Whatever reasoning I tried to do with myself, it didn't matter. I was stuck in jail. I put that voice of my mind in jail. I didn't want to hear its reasoning of why it felt that I should mope around like a turd.

After mulling over the pity party I was throwing for myself, I remembered what I had learned before all this crap happened. I learned to be selfless and more empathetic in dealing with others. I even knew that I shouldn't focus so much on the materials of life. But that didn't stop me from going down the hole of discouragement. What I hadn't understood or learned up to this point was to be compassionate with myself and to forgive myself for my actions.

If we can forgive others for their past, why couldn't I forgive myself? If you honestly think about that, how can you ever change or better yourself if you cannot forgive yourself? Others will forgive you in time, but you have to start with you.

So, I forgave myself for the past events and actions, then forgave others for my perceived deception they had towards me. The key here is to understand that just because you think someone may view you in a certain light, is that they probably don't. You're likely making it out to be bigger than it really is. The only way to truly know what they are thinking is to confront the situation and ask questions. If you're lied to and know it, so what. Move on and know that through forgiveness you can carry on with your life with or without them.

Why do we suffer

Even though I didn't care to die anymore at that time, I knew I needed to change my attitude and outlook. We all get the motivation taken out of our sails every now and then. Life will beat us all down eventually. That's usually an indicator that you need to discover the new you that's emerging from the depths of isolation. Through sufferings we find true meaning in what we are meant to do. What we have to do here on Earth is to do just that, suffer. We were made to suffer with all that is life. When I feel like dying now, I know that I am meant to suffer for a little while until I can emerge glorious again.

Otherwise, if I quit, I will not conquer this life's moments as we are all meant to. We have a purpose to never give up. To keep falling forward with a love to serve each other in a way that brings us closer together with more reverence in our interactions. Every second of our lives should be set serving each other in warm company while we are enjoying food and good times.

With that new perception, I decided to go on parole and release myself from my mind's jail. I forgave myself and started to understand I was meant for something else in this life. I mean, we are supposed to have a purpose, right? Otherwise, why are we here? Do you not think we have a purpose? Are we not meant for more than we think we are? How is it that we can only communicate with each other but not with any other of the millions of species on this planet? They seem to have a common language, but we cannot hear it. Evolution maybe? What if it's a feeling and not a noise?

Either way, who cares what the purpose of life truly is, but if you happen to give yourself a purpose then great, be satisfied with that. Enjoy your singular life. Speak whatever language you want to whatever you want as long as you feel a connection based on love with that other being.

If life feels undone to you because you are still searching for that purpose, then maybe it is? You may be caught up chasing the purpose of life in hopes that you'll accomplish something that will classify you as a winner. Here's a little secret, you'll never win!

You'll never be done until your life is done. Just because you accomplished something doesn't mean you've finished. There is no finish line in life. What line are you going to cross that you'll ever be satisfied with. Death?

Death finishes us all eventually. Some of us sooner than later. Those that go and seek it out will succumb to it in a relative time, trust me. Just because people die doesn't mean they are the weakest of the weak either. Some that die young may have pushed themselves harder and crossed physical boundaries that were not meant to be crossed. Also, I believe if you've made it to old age, you are not weak either. This life is hard and surviving to be an elder should be a privilege.

You have to be strong willed to make it through this life. You definitely won't make it out alive but if you can suffer through it better than most, you can make it a little more comfortable than it has been in your past. You'll never be done until you're done. In that sense you have to keep falling forward to the finish line of life.

Put effort into everything you do. Find your purpose. Your potential is calculated by the energy you put into the outcome. Go hard and be humble! Don't be scared of giving it your all.

I'll tell you one thing, I am much more afraid to live than I am to die. Dying is only one action. Living consists of a lot of shit that can cause pain and anguish, but also give a ton of pleasure. Life is an unknown length of time that you cannot judge and to me, that scares the shit out of me. It also makes me a little angry.

Though, with life, you can always change what's going on around you or who is involved in your life. If you get depressed and start thinking death is your only ticket out, think again. You always have the choice of change. You can literally run from your life. In certain circumstances that may just mean moving to another town or changing jobs. Maybe you don't care for the people around you? Run from them and surround yourself with those that make you happy. Do not think of death as being your one choice for change. Trust me, I know.

Even if you don't have the capability to actually change one of those aspects immediately, you can always find another way out. You could go for a run if you are able. You could also just disappear for a little bit. Get some time to yourself so you can run away from your emotions and all the bullshit that's dragging you down. Getting away from all the noise in your life should give you ample amount of time to reflect on what's bothering you and give you some time to make a plan for change. Stick to that plan! If you set a goal for yourself, stick to it. Make mini goals to help you complete the ultimate goal if that's what it takes but dammit, conquer that goal.

It once took me over 5 years to hit a goal of mine, but I knew it would take time to accomplish it when I set out for it. Just suffer through it.

What are you running from

Everything that was happening in my life those days was fueling my run. I was running with my emotions. All the craziness I felt inside was energy to get out and run. I was literally running away from my life for short periods of time before returning to my reality.

I realized I've been running my whole life and hadn't known it. I've ran from people I didn't enjoy being around or that I felt treated me badly. I ran away from home because I didn't like the rules. I ran away from my hometown because I couldn't fathom the thought of dying in that town and what everyone would say at my funeral. I've ran from toxic workplaces as well. I have to keep moving. I'm like a shark in the sense that if I stop moving, I feel I might die. I have to run!

Running, in the sense of the physical activity where you move your legs, has been the best resource for me to be able to clear my head. I can't keep moving from town to town and running away from all my problems.

For one, I enjoy solving problems and I now realize I have had the wrong approach to issues in my life. I have to stay and fight. That meant I needed an outlet, like going for a run or working out, to give me time away from the day to day distractions so I can figure out answers to all my problems. I can tell you that so far, it's going well. Running gives me time to make a plan of action for my issues. Having a plan is step one to trying to fix an issue. Otherwise, it will stay an issue.

For you, running may not be the key to your sanity but that doesn't mean you are not able to find something that gives you silence and peace of mind. What in your life do you enjoy? What gives you time to yourself to gather your thoughts? Whatever that may be, I suggest dedicating some "you" time so you can stay in the battle of life.

I've been using running to escape the reality of my life but that has only been a temporary fix. It's usually only short lived too. Instead of distracting myself, I realized I needed to become more focused. I needed to be more attentive and conscious. The only way that I have figured out to really escape the reality of my life, is to live in that reality. I get bored easily with reality. Especially when it becomes routine. I have to find things that are enjoyable and routine but also have a sense of unpredictability in them.

Running is completely unpredictable. Yes, you may know your route or how far you're going or how long it's going to take you, but you don't know what you're going to encounter. You could hurt yourself running by tripping or falling and spraining an ankle? You might get chased by a dog? You might meet the love of your life? You could also come up with new ideas or find a new route to take. That's what makes running so enjoyable. It's the action of moving full speed ahead into the unknown but eventually it comes to a known end. Hopefully, that is.

You may have a pre-determined and predictable time that you're running for and once that's over then you have to have something else on your schedule to do that brings joy into your life. It has to be interesting, intriguing and engaging. Otherwise, life becomes mundane and boring. You won't have the motivation to go out and get it done.

I have to try to invest in different activities in my life. Like signing up to coach my son's baseball league or being a Scoutmaster. Other ideas I've thought of to keep your mind at ease is to engage in your local community by signing up for classes at a recreation center or teaching something at a school. You'll end up talking to people you've never met. By engaging with people in your community, you will have more meaning in your life than the same old shit like getting up and going to work, coming home, cooking dinner and going to bed. Rinse wash repeat.

You can make a difference in your life and the lives of others, but only if you're present for it. I know we can all do great things. I can feel it. I can feel it about myself too. I have a feeling that there is something big out there waiting for me, but it may also be a small feat like making a stranger smile while out for a run. You never know. That simple show of gratitude in a warm smile may change that person's perspective in life. They may go forward from that day to achieve greatness that will change the world, just by the simple gesture of a smile.

Either way, I will take pride in knowing that I will one day achieve greatness. No matter how big or small it may be. I know I will make an impact on this Earth and help the beings I accompany it with.

Although none of that would be possible if I took the easy way out of life because of my selfishness. My focus and emotions needed to shift to release me from all the bullshit that held me down. I had to find myself by leaving everything that defined me behind. I realized that the less you care about the materials in your world, the freer you'll be. The less you have, the less you have to be concerned with and care about if you happen to lose it. Even what you have, realize it will go away one day. Like your job or ability to run. Don't get attached but rather, enjoy it while you have it. Count your blessings.

There was one thing that kept me going through it all. I can say for certain that it is undeniably the most powerful force in this universe, no not hate, it was love. Especially unconditional love. It doesn't care who you are or how you act, love is always there. I know that my kids love me unconditionally and I love them just the same, but stronger. I cannot give up and leave them hanging. I have to be present in their lives. I cannot check out and abandon my greatest creations. They are my proudest achievement. After acknowledging that, I woke the fuck up and quit shitting on myself for not believing in my abilities.

There's always this wave of resentment and self-loathing I've been riding, and I was ready to dive into the water of self-forgiveness. But this wouldn't be the last time these thoughts would cross my mind, nor would it be the last battle with myself.

I gave myself a good stern talking to one day to motivate me to fight back. I screamed at myself until I felt like I was worthy enough to carry on and leave discouragement in the dust. If you wallow around in your self-pity and beat yourself up for not being good enough, you'll never be good enough. You have to pick yourself up and try again. It may be scary at times, but you have to leave the hate for yourself at the door. Don't fear what the future may hold. Run towards it.

Chapter 7

Fear Not!

When it was mutually agreed upon that I needed to leave my job because it was not benefiting me or my place of employment, I was in a bad place. As I noted previously, I fell into darkness where I doubted myself and my ability. I didn't know what to do or how to handle the situation. One thing I knew for sure was that I wanted to give up. I was done. Done with life. I had a sinking feeling that I failed at life but more importantly that I failed my family. I would ask myself, "Did I move my family across the country and away from our hometown for this?" What was I to do? I was living in fear and with fear comes broad ranges of despair.

I had lost it. Mentally I was done. I didn't want to wake up anymore. I didn't want to carry on with my job anymore. I didn't care about my vehicle or the clothes I wore. I was, and still am, tired of trying to find good shoes, reliable transportation or a steady job. I had lost the will to fight for things that everyone else says matters the most.

Why should I continue? Because it's not about me! I had lost the will to carry on with the remaining time I have left on Earth, because I don't care for the inevitable failure from all these materialistic items that I had become attached to. I'm tired of having to seek out another materialistic item that I deem worthy of the original. There's no going back for what you've lost. The past is gone.

Some of us fear that fear. You know, the feeling that you can't go back home. That feeling that all of your memories are all that you have of your past. To me, there's nothing more frightful than losing everything you have, even your memories.

Fear is a powerful sense of feeling. It cripples us into believing we are not capable of succeeding. Fear crushes our hopes and dreams into pieces of dust that get blown away by the wind of life. Fear stops us from completing our goals even after we've started down the path of redemption. This extraordinary emotion can consume our entire personality and state of being.

Just as with hate, we are not born being fearful. This action is something we had to learn and have been conditioned into since we were children. The never-ending warnings about how something bad will happen if we proceed with our obviously dangerous idea that we tried to put into action, is always there to scare us. Of course, knowing the difference between a bad idea and one that we should be cautious about is something a child cannot grasp at an early age. Nevertheless, we have been coaxed into fearing the "what ifs" to a point that it shields us from performing certain tasks in life.

For instance, people fear how others will judge them if they do something not deemed acceptable in society. We are fearful that we will be banished into the underworld of society if we break those golden rules. Dare we stand out?

What if I wore my hair a different way than usual? Will I be laughed at? Will I lose all my friends? What about all the hateful stuff people will say about me behind my back?

Our minds get consumed with the fear of not being accepted to the point that we will not change for the lack of will it takes to accept ourselves. Though I will note, don't try to be someone you're not. A year before I left this last job, I started to grow my hair out. I was so desperate for change that I thought, if I could grow my hair out, I could be someone else. Someone more likable than the angry turd I was acting like. I was dead wrong, again. Growing my hair out eventually made me lose all self confidence in myself. Every day I judged myself. I wasn't who I wanted to be. I struggled every day not to cut my hair until one day, I'd had enough. I couldn't stand the mullet. Me with long hair isn't who I am. I hated how I looked. How I looked meant a lot to my self-esteem.

If you are not being your true self, you will never be happy or confident in what you know and how you project yourself. I was trying to be someone I was not. Which was a person living in constant fear of how I was perceived every day I kept that mullet. I was trying to imitate other people and their style. Screw that. I ain't them. I am who I am!

I gained so much more confidence when I decided to get back to my old clean-cut haircut. I had a style and it was original to me. Plus, I looked like some old man from the 80s with my long hair. Ewe! Maybe if I had a mustache with the haircut, I would have had more confidence?

I literally feared what I had become as a perception in everyone's mind. That struck fear within me and limited my interactions with people in social situations. I will say one thing. It takes a ton of mental toughness to grow your hair out and deal with what you believe everyone else is thinking of you. You are constantly judging yourself, your motives and everyone's opinion of you. You have to overcome so many mental games. It will beat you down. For me, I felt like I overcame the stigma and decided to get back to being who I knew who I was.

Other examples of fear are those in which we do not trust ourselves. We don't trust that our body and mind are capable of such tasks to the point that we just give up.

This can go back to the mentality of a child in certain situations. We may not know how to do something perfectly, so we don't even attempt it. Take food for example. How many times have you decided not to eat something because it was different or looked weird? If you have kids, hopefully you can relate to that. Just like a stubborn kid who won't try apple sauce for the first time because it looks like some mysterious gray mush, we too do not branch out because of our own fears of what the experience may turn out to be. Another "what-if" we tell ourselves to psych ourselves out.

There's nothing that will change your mind on trying octopus tentacle, right? I mean why even attempt to try it. I'm sure it tastes just like it looks, which is gross. It's really not that bad but it is chewy like you would imagine.

Our mind is being fearful of the unknown. We tell ourselves, "What will happen if I do that? I shouldn't even attempt it due to the fact that I cannot conceive any reactions from me acting on such a task. What if I don't do it right? What if it tastes weird and I have to spit it out in front of people? If I fail, what will everyone think of me once I'm deemed a failure."

We have a lack of faith in ourselves and a fear of the future when doing everyday tasks. We don't want to be judged but then we judge ourselves to the point that we never attempt what we may be passionate about. You have to let go and open your mind to the possibility that the unknown will give you grace in discovering something new. Don't fear what you've never done before because it could be the best thing you've ever experienced.

What's the worst that can happen

There are so many ways that we induce fear in ourselves or have fear bestowed upon us from external sources. People and random acts of fuckery seem to poke at us from time to time with a purpose to induce some sort of fear. Their intentions may be to induce fear in a way that redirects us into a different direction or maybe they just want to pick on us and show how important they are. You have to maintain a collective and rational disposition when this happens. Otherwise, you could lose your shit and be lost even more into this world of fear.

Hell, I didn't want to publish this book. I'm fearful of the response from our social society. I'm fearful of the opinions people will have of my opinions. What if I lose all that I hold as precious to me? What if my family rejects me? What if I lose my job and am never able to obtain another because of what people think I am?

With all the scare tactics used by our news and media outlets to boost their ratings, I cannot see how more people don't have anxiety about what people think about them or what they say. Shit I'm scared to eat for the fear of catching one in a hundred different variants of cancer they talk about on the news every day.

That kind of thinking scares the shit out of me and makes me unable to move forward with a lot of aspects in my life. I'm fearful of moving forward so I remain standing still. I'd rather just wither away into a life lived in darkness, but I can't.

If I want to move forward, I have to not give a damn about the outside influence that our social society lays upon us all. I cannot give into the negativity that comes with change.

What if an Artist never released their paintings, music or ideas because they were fearful of other's opinions? We never would have experienced their beliefs or cultural influences in their lives. That knowledge is precious if we want to grow as human beings. You cannot let outside pressure of negative responses knock you off course. You have to go for it. You have to become stronger than you think you are and know that you are in control. Just put yourself out there.

We have to live like a Hawk. We have to act like a predator instead of like the prey. Next time someone or something is poking you to invoke fear in you, try to remember to be like a Hawk. Hawks are fearless. Have you ever witnessed a Hawk being attacked by other smaller birds? Hawks are calm. They could care less about the other birds swooping down trying to attack them while they are flying through the air.

Those other birds act frantically and try to scare the Hawk away so it will get out of its area. All the while the hawk is laser focused. Focused on his goal. Finding a means to an end. He's determined to hunt for what he desires.

You can learn a lot by watching wildlife and spending time in the wilderness. It's great for your mental health to go for a walk in the woods. Plus, it's super quiet. Sometimes we just need some peace and quiet. The wilderness has that but also the added benefit of nature's natural beauty and the flow of life.

The few times I've seen a Hawk get attacked by other birds, it's been a revelation in emotional competency. The ability to ignore those who seem to want to hurt you and do harm towards you is phenomenal. Being able to block them out while staying on point is imperative to your emotional stability. Do not let external sources deter you or bring you down to their level. Stay above them on the high road to success.

In this life we have a choice. We can act rash and pay the consequences or stay calm and get what we're after.

There are really only two kinds of lives you can live. One that is fruitful and one that is not. You get to choose what you do with your gift of life. You can choose to live every day in fear of what everyone thinks, or say fuck it, and go make shit happen. You can choose to help others by lifting them up and bringing them cheer or happiness into their life.

On the flip side, instead of showing them love, you could decide not to be fruitful and be a vengeful, deceitful, conniving, and a downright piece of shit. You have the choice to do good or do bad. To produce fruit or rot on the vine. Choose wisely because you only have one chance at it. That revelation right there should be enough to change your life for the good.

This frame of mind of being fearful is yet another hurdle that we must overcome before we can be fully happy and start to enjoy life in a manner that boosts our self-confidence to the point that we do not care about the reactions from external influence we obtain in our everyday lives. Fear does not just occur. It is created by our own reality. Being fearful inhibits you from enjoying life. Take a second and try to remember some of those times in your life when you were scared to act upon something. Could you have handled it better? Would going against your fear have been beneficial or did you happen to make the right decision?

How do you use fear

Our fear controls us. It guides us and sometimes, misleads us. But you have to know when you screwed up and admit you made a mistake so you can get back on course. Also don't let the fear we have for others deter you from taking the path you want to take. We fear that something bad will happen or come about if someone did certain actions towards us while we're on our path, right? Or better yet, have you ever stopped someone from going down the path they were charting because you were fearful for them?

For example, have you noticed a loved one or a complete stranger about to attempt something that could cause grave harm to them mentally or physically and tried to stop them? This could be as simple as moving away from home or as crazy as jumping off a bridge into a fast-moving river current. Yeah, I've done both. Each instance was invigorating. You never know how you will actually feel until you go and do it. No one ever tried to stop me but I'm sure they didn't think it was a great idea.

Though there are times when stopping someone, or yourself, from going down the wrong path is a good thing. Take for instance an example that you just realized that you or someone else was hooked on drugs and you knew that they, or you, should get backhanded right away as if to steer them, or yourself, back on the straight and narrow.

We try to instill fear into others so they will not act on their intentions. I'm sure that if I told my Mother that I was about to go jump off a bridge into a swift river current or go do drugs, that she would freak out and try to stop me, but in actuality she's just trying to keep me safe. We are ultimately trying to keep everyone we love safe by scaring them. We need to stop that!

You have to let go and let people learn for themselves. We can only understand the true meaning of what we are chasing once we discover it for ourselves. Sometimes that's not the right way to learn but maybe it's a necessity for some of us to feel the results of our actions. Words cannot do it justice in our mind's reality. Although, if someone is bad off on drugs, don't give up on them. Try to get them back on track. Drugs, all forms, are bad long term.

There is also this! We create fear in others for the sole purpose to control them for our benefit and not just for the benefit of them. This comes back to my point about being told to not do something because it's in the best interest of the one who's condemning you. An example would be telling a child that they shouldn't do something because it was bad. Something so innocent as telling a child that he will get a spanking if he makes that stupid sound again or if they keep banging on the table with that fork, that it will end in a bad situation. In that instance we are not fearing what will happen to them or their safety if they do something bad but rather bestowing fear upon them because they are behaving a certain way that we disagree with.

We want to control things through the use of fear. This type of example is used too frequently on adults. Can you think of a time when you've been pushed into a direction due to fear and it ultimately benefited someone else?

We need to stop worrying about what everyone else thinks about how we are or what we do. We need to stop dishing out fear as a solution to our problems. Fear has become a cycle that holds us and others back from excelling. We need to know our own limits of our own physical and mental capabilities. We cannot be simply told about the experience but rather we need to know it firsthand. The only thing that will suffice is our own personal experience. If it turns out to be a bad decision, then hopefully you can admit your faults and reconcile with your opposition.

This is not owning to fear for the lack of ability but rather knowing yourself wholly and what we are capable of handling. That is so we can safely say, "My body and mind cannot go any further." There are these physical and mental thresholds we hit every day and some of us have higher or low thresholds than others. That's why we tend to disregard others' suggestions and take matters into our own hands. We all have limits and an urge to learn the boundaries of the vessel we inhabit.

How much can you take

Sometimes we think there are physical thresholds but in reality, it's are our own mind's way of telling us it's had enough. It cannot fathom what happens next. What happens if I keep going? Will I die? This is not fear but the mind's way of saying you've hit a mental barrier and that we may need to stop. The mind freaks out when it gets to a point that it's never reached before. The body is capable of much more than the mind believes.

I've been to the point of physical and mental exhaustion to where I believed I could go no further and thought "This was THE END, just give up." Although many times, I would just push forward with disregard of fear and the consequences of what happened next. I didn't care what people thought of me if I broke myself. I honestly did not care what the outcome was. I had been through enough and was ready to take more.

In those times I would ask myself, "Am I not afraid? Do I have no fear?" No, I had not lost all fear nor was I not afraid. I was curious. I wanted to see how far I could go. I wanted to believe that I was stronger than I thought I was. I wanted to know where the boundary between life and death lived. I will not bow to fear's empowering feeling but instead simply let go and embrace the unknown.

This may or may not be a good alternative to fear, letting go, but it was my start to a happier life. I cannot control other people and how they view me. I cannot control the consequences to my actions if I have never experienced the action before. I can only control my own reality of things and my reactions to them. My reality is based on personal experiences. Whether good or bad, they drove me to where I am today. I realized that by letting go of outside influences that I could reduce my fear to a tiny fraction of what I used to be fearful of. I needed to believe in myself again and let go at the same time.

Letting go by trusting in yourself and trusting in what you're capable of is where it all starts. The beginning of my life had just begun. I was willing to try new things. I will wear stylish and hip clothes. I will try new exotic foods. I will go to new places and explore their wonders. I will have no fear of the unknown!

Repeat after me. I know that giving up is a decision of my mind and not my body. Though, if my body and mind are not fit or privy to the truth, then none of this is true. I must realize what my reality entails. I must be aware of my surroundings. I must determine my limits and thresholds through personal experiences where I have pushed beyond fear. I am capable of doing anything to the point of breaking or bending my mental and physical wellbeing. Fear will not stop me for fear is a figment of my creation. If I do not recognize it as being true, then it will not exist in my reality.

I'll tell you this; I do not understand the course of my life but I am grateful for it's trajectory. I had always feared I would die young. I never thought I'd live past 22. Even when I turned 23, I still didn't believe I'd make it past 25.

Then again, once I turned 26 I didn't think I'd live past 29. To this day I still believe I will die young but I'm not fearful of death much anymore. Maybe my problem is that I cannot see myself mastering old age or for that matter, getting to an older age. It's hard to imagine our future but it shouldn't be frightening to not be able to imagine the unknown. We can chart a great path if we put in the effort but if we sit still in fear of not wanting to move forward then nothing will happen.

I am grateful for every day I have. Every day I have with my kids. Even those days when I really do not want to be an adult, interact with anyone, be a father or a loving husband, I force myself to participate in life.

Life is an experiment. One that could have grave consequences without a little bit of fear. All my life I have tried different methods, tactics and ideologies to see if any of them work or are true in any way to me. All of those experiments have led to my accumulation of experience through self-discovery. To live with fear, and at times without, can create opportunities that we wouldn't have seen coming. You never know when something will work out for the best. You have to take a chance whether you're fearful or not. Again, life is an experiment.

Think about taking vitamins or supplements. Have you ever taken any to help your body recover or heal? You're experimenting with yourself in hopes that the outcome is good even though you truly have no idea what the outcome may be, right? You may or may not have a positive outcome from the vitamin. But nonetheless, you are a little skeptical of what could happen after you swallow that pill, right? You may have an allergic reaction? It may very well help you in some manner, but you will never know if you don't assume the risk of the experiment and set aside your fear.

Seeing as I've never been a Human before, I feel like it's my duty to experiment. We have to find out just how far our body and mind can go. For that to happen, you have to let go of the fear within you long enough to peer over to the other side. Play the game and take chances.

You also have to play like you're never winning. This is a very long game of chess we're playing, and it may take multiple games until it's over. No matter how many times you win or lose, you have to play until the game of life is over. If you win along the way, give yourself a nice high five and move on. Never count your accomplishments. If you are satisfied with winning one challenge you will not be able to win a second because that takes drive. Being satisfied and proud with your success will not motivate you to chase after other opportunities to win. You have to be hungry!

There's a difference between winning something and dominating it. Winning is something you get lucky doing once or twice but dominating is knowing you have it in you to last until time runs out.

When it comes to running and racing or even working out with your normal routine, you have to be able to give it your all until your predetermined time runs out or the time for the allotted session is gone. That's being a competitor.

When it comes to the game or race of life, it's a mental game. If you want to live a long time you have to be mentally prepared to go the distance until your time runs out. I had wanted to give up many times in my life and in many different aspects, but I had never quit, and I never intend to.

When a man is stretched to the end of his will and has lost everything, he becomes tired. When a man is tired, he will do anything to rest. Beware the man who has lost everything and is ready to rest because he has also lost his fear. He will fight like the most savage of beasts until he can rest.

Part Four:

The Ugly Truth

Chapter 8

Turning off the Want Machine

Happiness from sadness to depression into hope, then greed from anger out of fear. The thought behind our flow of emotions is that they are born of each other. For instance, we may fear something and decide that, to get over our fear we should get angry at it to the point that we build up enough courage, or power, to overcome it. Once we are sufficiently angry or filled with enough ego, we tend to like it and want more. Call it being greedy.

I had some time on my hands between jobs that gave me time to reflect, once again, back on my life. I realized I had been greedy my whole life. My conclusion to how I happened upon this time and place that I'm in, was because of my ambitions. I wanted.

I wanted a good life for my family. To me that meant living in a modest house with nice clothes, enough healthy food to eat, nice furnishings and reliable transportation to get us out of the house every now and then. The "good life" I wanted for my family wasn't all materialistic. No, I wanted us to be happy and live together in peace and love. I wanted us to be able to respect one another and talk freely about our issues, if we had any.

I wanted my children to be successful, or at least one day the opportunity to be. Whether they turned out that way or not, I had to make sure they had every possible opportunity for success. That's why the Wife and I moved across the county. I had to make sure our children had the best opportunity for a rock-solid education and the least chance for suburban crime activity. I wanted our children to live in a safe area and grow up in an environment that was conducive to their future success.

I also wanted to be renowned for my intelligence within my career. I wanted to be known to the world for what I knew and what I was capable of achieving. I wanted to be famous. Famous to me wasn't about being a movie star, musician or comedian. I wanted to be a famous CEO or someone else who's highly regarded in their industry. I wanted to be special. I know now that all those things that

I wanted were selfish. I wanted all these things for myself. Not once did I ask anyone what they wanted.

Now that's not to say I was fully immersed in my selfishness, because what I wanted some of the time was for the benefit of someone else.

I wanted my Wife and kids to be happy and have all the stuff they ever wanted. So, I tried advancing my career many times over to make more money and buy things to make them happy.

I also worked on being likable and funny so people could feel good about themselves when they were around me, especially my family. I even wanted a well-paying job that gave me the opportunity to flourish within or from outside of the company boundary, so I could make them look good by representation. I wanted to be so smart so I could help out anyone in need. So much so that I would be remembered for centuries well after my death for all the good I did.

Want want want. I realized I had a hole in me that I couldn't fill.

When will you be full

You may think that all of my wants were reasonable. I thought they were. I didn't think anything of them. That is until I stepped back from my life to realize, I was never satisfied after getting what I wanted. Nor would I ever be satisfied if I ever achieved some of my more elaborate wants, like fame and fortune. I knew deep down that my wants only gave me something to drive towards. They were not fulfilling anything. I truly had a hole in me. A deep dark hole that was consuming my time on Earth and misleading me from the important things in life.

Let's talk about that hole within us all. That emptiness that you feel inside you. You may not know it's there, but we all try to search for something to fill that hole. At times it feels as though we keep pushing things in but never seem to close it up. We keep stuffing shit in it over and over again, until the process of filling that hole blinds us from seeing what we actually have.

We are greedy. If we get something that makes us feel good for a little bit, we keep going after it. We have to have more of it. We need one of every color or flavor. We need it to survive.

What are some of the things you chase after? In what ways do you repeat the process of satisfying your hunger for success and happiness? Do you consistently buy the same things over and over? Do you take chances gambling your paycheck away? Do you have a habit of doing the same thing every day but never feel whole? In what ways are you trying to fill that hole within you? There are a lot of ways that we try to feel satisfied and fulfill the hole within all of us.

Let's use chocolate as an example. We love it in society. At least some people do. For some of us, when we don't have our evening chocolate delight because we've accidentally run out, we have to go run and get some before it's too late. And you'll do anything to get some chocolate. You would drive 30 minutes down the road just to get some 80% cocoa dark chocolate. You just have to have it. Once you get the opportunity to replenish your stock, you might as well buy as much as you can because nobody else needs to have chocolate but you, right? What if you happen to run out tomorrow? You have to at least get enough to last you through the week or maybe even until the end of the month. You're the only one that needs chocolate here. Nobody else matters!

Obviously, you can replace chocolate with many other things. This is just an example but let your mind fill in the blanks about what other things can consume us. What about coffee? How many of you have to have coffee before you can do anything? Heaven forbid you skip your morning coffee. How would you make it through the day?

Here's another example, shoes. How many of you out there have a thing for shoes? You have to have the latest and most popular brand of shoes hitting the market. You also let your family and friends know how amazing those shoes are and boast about your procurement. But once the shine of those new shoes wears off, you have to get a new pair and the old shoes sit on a shelf never to be worn again. You're always chasing after the next fresh pair of shoes. What about the ones you bought previously? Do they not matter anymore? Are they not as important as the new shoes? Do they not match the style of your clothes anymore?

My point is that we get so enthralled in the emotion of wanting, or greed, that it consumes us. It drives our life's decisions. If we can't get what we want, scratch that, no we're greedy. We always get what we want. We will always get what we want as long as we are patient enough! No matter how long it takes, we'll keep driving towards our goals of obtaining the newest object marketed to us. One day, you'll have all that you want!

It's really not that bad to have a goal of obtaining something but just make sure it's something that will give you long lasting happiness. Like, a degree from an accredited college, a lifelong lover or friend, a business decision that changes the world or just some simple quiet time away from the hustle and bustle of the world.

The thing is some of us live our entire lives not realizing how consumed we are with things we want. There is no limit to how much of it we have because we have to have it to live. It's more important to us than oxygen. This process of wanting all the time is what I like to call, The Want Machine.

You want and you want, and you want, and you want. It's reminiscent of the sound of a child. I want this Mama. I want that Daddy. I want want want want. And to be quite honest, it's annoying to other people. We are really just children if you think about it. We never actually grow up. Yes, maybe we do look and talk like an adult but are we really? My Wife jokes that I'm her oldest child and to be honest, I am. The only difference between my children and me is that I get what I want and don't have to whine for it. Most of those things I want are really "needs" though. I need certain things to keep my family safe, fed and happy.

Take a look back and reflect on points in your life where greed had consumed you to the point where nothing else mattered. Nobody else mattered except for your wants. What was that goal of obtaining whatever it was? Did you sacrifice relationships? Have you sacrificed a career over it? Have you even sacrificed all of your belongings just to get what you want? Did you throw away everything in your life just to get what you wanted?

How is it that we can be so consumed with our wants that we forget what we already have? Sometimes the things we already have just need to be polished up to be made new again.

Is it grit or is it greed

There is this misconception that greedy people are always successful. You know that is a lie. Because greed is not what a lot of people think it is. It's an addiction. You can't stop feeling that emptiness inside you. Nothing will satisfy your wants. You're like a black hole in the universe consuming everything around you and everything you can get your hands on. There is no end to your wants.

Successful people may have that hole but let's try to realize that they might not be greedy. Give them the benefit of the doubt by saying that they have the drive to see things through to the end until they get what they want! They have invested time on things for the benefit of their future and the future of others. They wanted tangible things and figured out a way to obtain it. Call it greed. Call it drive. Call it patience. Call it grit. There is a big ol' nasty pothole there and it needs to be filled in every few weeks. We all have a hole that needs to be filled.

I will say, there's a fine line between grit and greed. One continuously drives towards the same object over and over but the other only wants that one thing once, and after it's achieved, it goes out to conquer something new. Let's be clear. There is a difference! One's healthy and one's not.

If you get hung up chasing the same thing over and over, it may be an addiction. If you can't sit still and have to discover new things or constantly try new things, that's ok. That doesn't mean you don't respect or take for granted those things in life that make you happy. Some classify that as having attention deficit disorder. All I'm saying is, be careful not to fall into the dark side of ambition. We all have grit and want to conquer things.

Make sure it's for the right reasons and if it's not, work on a little self-control. You are in charge. Not your mind.

I have always wanted things. I wanted them so badly and worked so hard for them that I thought that if I didn't obtain it, it was the end of the world. My greed and obsession with obtaining it led to my defeat. My mind was telling me this was the only way to happiness. I wasn't chasing the same thing over and over but rather only one goal at a time. When I didn't obtain my wants in life, I was consumed with sadness and depression and the feeling of being worthless from not accomplishing my goal. And that's the problem with the want machine.

If you want it so badly that you feel like your life depends on it but don't ever get it, your mind will go into a state of distress. It can lead you into a state of sadness and fear of what could happen if you don't get what you want. What if you don't get what you want? I'll admit that sometimes this feeling can lead to suicidal thoughts. Don't get caught in that trap.

I felt that way when I was unemployed. I truly didn't get what I wanted out of life and was depressed about it. I'm sure other people on this planet have felt the same way. Maybe not over the same situation but over a similar one, I'm sure. Have you or a loved one ever become so distraught over not getting what you wanted in life that you or someone you know have attempted or committed suicide? It's sad to realize how powerful our wants can be. We set the expectation of them that if they do not appear in our lives, that there's no point in living anymore. What kind of madness is that? Let it be people!

You will get what you get. So, don't throw a fit. To overcome greed and the pitfalls that come from not getting what we want, make a list of all that you have and rank them from the highest priority to the lowest priority. Rank them from things that you can't live without and then make a list of things you can leave behind. You should notice that you have all the things that are important to you and that all the things you want are secondary. They are not truly important in life. They are nice to have but not a necessity.

Throughout my life I've encountered greedy people, and they seem happy. Because at that point in time in their life, they have what they want. They shove it into their hole long enough to trick us that they are happy. But that's not really reality now, is it? Your mind will play tricks on you if you let it. Stay sharp in your discernment.

Whatever it is that you decided you want and you're dead set on getting it, your mind will make you think that that's the right decision. It agrees with you and tells you that that's what you should be doing. It tells you that this thing is what you need to survive and prosper. But in all honesty your mind is the worst enemy in the world. It will agree with you no matter what decision you rationalize in your head as being the right one. It just wants to be right. This is where you have to know the difference between you and your mind. Your control plane versus your data plane. This is where you learn that you can have self-control.

Who's really in charge

Your mind is like the devil. It's there to trick you into thinking you are right because it wants to be right. It will agree with you no matter what as long as you feel good about the decision.

Have you ever heard about the two wolves battling in each of us? One is a good wolf and the other one is a bad wolf. Which one wins? Whether it's good for you or not, it will be the one you feed the most.

The thing about the mind is that it alone, in essence, is greedy. It wants all these things for you. It wants you to be happy. It NEEDS all these things. It convinces you to think that these things are going to make you happy, but the truth is, your mind wasn't there in the beginning when you were a baby or young child.

Your mind learned from society about things in this world and how they can satisfy you. When you were a baby that voice wasn't there or even created yet. As a baby, could you speak any languages? That voice in your head that controls all your thoughts hadn't developed to tell you what you wanted. You got handed a block, or a cardboard box, and thought it was the coolest thing in the world. After your first good experience with those objects, you needed it and had to have it all the time because it gave you great pleasure. That is until you found something else that gave you a better experience. Then you moved on and forgot what you had to begin with.

Think about that voice in your head for a moment and recall the example from the beginning of the book where I had you imagine looking at a sunset over the mountains. Remember what I said about that little voice in your head and how it didn't have to tell you how orange the sunset was or how purple the hue over the mountains were. You already knew about the colors and beauty of it all. That voice wasn't there to confirm what you already knew.

That voice in your head is the source of all your problems. If you focus hard enough, you may be able to muffle it so you can enjoy being satisfied with all that you have that is actually important to you.

As a society, to defeat this greed, this want machine inside us all, we need to let go of our importance of these Earthly possessions. We need to shut down the want machine. Just let go and not worry about what you have or don't have in your life. Maintain what you actually need in your life to survive. I'm not saying to give up everything and be as uncomfortable as possible. You can most definitely live a minimalist life but no, I'm saying be rational about what you need to live. Live a humble life that is not filled with this want. You'll get what you need.

When the slope becomes slippery

Being greedy only has two outcomes. Either you go back down the hole to a state of anger and land in fear of what-ifs from not getting what you want, or you'll start to hope. Once you get the feeling of hope, it may take a strong enough hold to where all you do is hope for what you want. Then greed sets back in to fulfill your hopes and dreams. You can't hope enough to overcome your issues.

Hope is a voided place. It's like purgatory. It takes action to move on from hope. If you fail to move past hope, the greed side of hope wins, and you get angry from all that doesn't work out and eventually become fearful that the world is against you. That could lead to some seriously demented actions.

Hope will put your expectations high. Don't let that happen. It will lead to sadness or greed or something completely new. Keep your expectations reasonable.

On the other hand, what if you retain your hope and stay in that void until the point where you realize nothing is coming from wishful thinking, you may get discouraged? Discouragement is a beast unto itself. It is Satan's most prized tool in his toolbox of destruction. It's tough to get past it. You may tend to fall back into hoping things will get better and maybe they do for a while, so you keep hoping due to the greed of wanting things to be better. We all know what happens next. You get angry that nothing ever works out and fall into being fearful of living. If that happens, the only thing you will want is for it all to end. It can be a vicious cycle if you let it be. Just stop wanting!

Another probable outcome could be, you could grieve for your depression from not getting what you want, and just be sad. Being sad is normal, but if left to sulk, you will fall back into a depression and sink back down into your hole of hope until fear takes hold of your emotional responses again. Though if you grieve and decide to move on from your troubles and realize that life is full of temporary moments, you will find happiness. Learn to let go and not fester. You can fail and most likely will. Don't worry about it. Learn from your failure and keep falling forward. Only you can get yourself out of the hole that you've thrusted yourself into.

Chapter 9

Climb out of that hole

If I lost you with my ramblings, that's okay. Let's recap. At this point in my life, I am a happily married 30 something year old man with two kids who moved his family across the country for a once in a lifetime job opportunity in hopes that I can build a bright future for all of us. I changed jobs again to what I thought was a better opportunity but then had to separate from my employer because I was an asshole and was left with some time to justify or condemn my previous actions that lead me up to this point in my life. Wow. This book could have been shorter.

It has been a great life altering time but after a couple months with no job, I only had one thing I could do besides sit back and shit on my past. I had to get out of the hole I was in. When you find yourself in a hole, the first thing you have to do is to stop digging.

While I was contemplating my life and trying to figure out what I should do with myself, I faced the fact that I needed a job. Priority number one was to find a job. Otherwise, if I didn't move quick enough, I would have to sell my house, file for bankruptcy and figure out how to support my family. That is, if my Wife didn't divorce me and take the kids with her, along with every last penny we had, back to Mississippi. As I noted earlier, I was in a state of mind to give up on life. I wanted nothing more than the pain and suffering to stop.

That's when I got mad. I somehow got so filled with resentment and anger over myself, that I ended up finding my light in the midst of darkness. I was mad at myself for letting this happen to me. I was the cause of my own demise. "What was I going to do about it?", I asked myself. I decided to get uncomfortable. I did the only thing I could do at the time to get uncomfortable and that meant being uncomfortable physically. So, I started working out harder. I wanted to punish myself through physical exertion. I needed to see how far I could go physically until I couldn't take it anymore, and then, go harder. I didn't want to be able to move the next day but also didn't know what would happen if I kept pushing harder.

That fear of the unknown I was experimenting with. I needed to break my mind.

Not only did I start lifting heavier and going harder in my workouts, but I would do just about anything to feel miserable. Just the thought of physical exertion and the pain I would feel the next day from being so sore that I could barely walk, was bliss to me.

I still had my initiative of finding new employment but what I needed the most at that point in time was a distraction. Something that would kill the pain long enough that I could rationalize with myself instead of reacting on emotions. I know for some out there, a distraction means drugs and alcohol. You know that's not the answer and I knew that too. Pain on the other hand was the next best thing for me.

Although, I knew it wasn't something I could keep doing long term because at some point I was bound to hurt myself from over doing it right? Yep. I needed a real plan. Something long term.

I set some goals to keep me in the race of life. Something to drive towards. Something to live for. So, I started planning what I would accomplish in the coming year. After figuring out what my options were that would keep me engaged longer than a day, I settled on spending my time studying for new industry certifications to replace the ones I already had but were about to expire. In addition to that, I decided I wanted to run a marathon. I'm not sure why I thought that was a good idea since I fucking hate running but it was a challenge none the less. One of those two goals I had done many times before and the other, well, was something I couldn't fathom. You can take a guess, but I'll just tell you. I had never run a marathon before.

Although I have had certifications in my field of study before, I had never obtained the highest degree of certifications classified as "expert". I always stayed at the level of certification that didn't take a whole lot of time, effort and money. It was reasonable. At least that's what I told myself. In truth, I was being lazy. I know myself too well. I don't like to put in much effort, but I want it all.

Well, that has never worked out for me and never will. I know that by now.

Both goals would challenge my mental and physical abilities and I was sure that one of them was my answer to move forward in life. I needed something else to do other than hurt myself with brutal and challenging workouts.

Who is this opportunity that's knocking

Before I could embark on my newfound plan, and while distracting my reality long enough with intense workouts so I could overcome the funk I was in, I had an acquaintance contact me about a job opening they had at his company. Pure luck here but I had been wanting to work for that company for a long time at that point. I tried at least 5 times previously to get a position there but never had the skills to make the cut. Being able to land a job at that company would be the pinnacle of my career. I won't lie, this opportunity gave me a glimmer of hope. Although I had been down that road before and knew not to set my expectations high. I had a good feeling about it, but I was still too numb inside to gauge if this opportunity was a possibility. I really didn't know what I was feeling to be honest, but I had a suspicion that the opportunity could help me out, given the situation I was in. I decided to play it cool. Whatever happened would happen. "Let it be.", I told myself.

I ended up getting the job. Heck yeah! It was my dream job. It didn't matter what my role was at the company, I was just happy to be working there.

With my new job came a little bit of time I could dedicate to studying for those expert level certifications. I also had some free time to add to my ruthless workout routine in the mornings. Since I would be working from home and didn't have to account for commuting time, I was free for an hour before I had to be online and working. This gave me a ton of time to get shit done in the mornings.

With all this extra time in the mornings, I decided I needed to try running again. Since one of my goals was to complete a marathon in the following year, this was a great time to start training.

Now, I hadn't ran in almost a year since my knee injury. I was being super cautious when it came to running because I didn't really want to relive the process of getting healthy again. That of which entailed six months of stretching to relieve the pain in my knee and a few more months on top of that convincing myself I was good to go.

Although, if I didn't attempt to run, I would never be able to train for the marathon. I decided to test the waters and see where I was at with my running abilities after not running for a while. Dip my toes in you could say.

I started out by running a mile. It was horrific. I was in shit sandwich shape. I felt like a turd before, during and after each run I completed. I hate running. It takes a ton of will power for me to get past the first couple of miles, or for that matter, to go running at all.

After three weeks of running every other day, I finally got back to being able to run a 5k without walking and gasping for air the entire time. I felt good, but it wasn't good enough for me. I was getting comfortable. I didn't like to be comfortable anymore. I found peace in being uncomfortable. "Give me pain and sweet misery!", I told myself. Oh, sweet misery...

Like any rational human being, I decided to throw down a challenge to myself and do a mock triathlon, but only half. I mean, I'm ambitious and all but come on. I know my limits. It was only a half triathlon!? I mean, what's the worst that could happen?

It wasn't a bad idea at the time, so I thought. How hard can it be? I did the math and found out what was all involved in a regular triathlon. For a standard full triathlon, the swimming portion is about 1.5km, the biking is 40km and the running is 10km. Well, I had a spin bike and a treadmill, but I didn't have a pool. Dilemma I know but I was determined.

I needed to find an alternative to swimming. I figured roughly how many arm strokes were involved in swimming and decided to do pushups to replace the swimming part. I'm sure I could have done rowing instead of push-ups but whatever. They both suck. I just chose one.

As I stated before, I really only wanted to do half of the triathlon distance just to see if I could accomplish it. Again, just testing the waters. What I came up with for the mockup of a half triathlon without swimming was to do 30 pushups every minute for 10 minutes for a total of 300 pushups. Then get on the spin bike and give it hell for 12 miles and after that hop on the treadmill for 3.1 miles. I was in semi good shape and this challenge seemed reasonable to me. Time consuming but reasonable.

So began my journey to test the waters and push myself harder after feeling comfortable doing 5k runs for a few weeks. This was my middle ground.

On the day I decided to try this out, I made sure I had ample free time to complete it all. As planned, I started out doing push-ups first. The push-ups weren't so bad and went by quickly. At that point I was pretty fair at doing push-ups. After the push-ups, I quickly got onto the spin bike and cranked the resistance. "Hell Yeah! Time to get to work.", I told myself. For 30 minutes I pedaled my ass off to put in the 12 miles needed for half the triathlon bike section. Once I crushed that, I jumped onto the treadmill. I felt good. I wasn't tired at all. I'm sure If I actually had a pool to do the swimming part, I would have been beat by the time it came to putting in the few miles running. Either way, I was close to finishing my task I set for myself, and I felt strong.

At the 2 mile mark of the last leg of my homemade mock half triathlon, my Wife calls me. She doesn't just call me once, but she starts blowing my phone up. Back to back calls. Then I started to hear my doorbell ring. "What the hell is going on?", I told myself and continued to curse. "Dammit I'm almost done with this exercise. Just give me ten minutes, come on!" Well, I thought the worst and answered my phone. I asked my Wife, "What happened? Did someone die?" Nope. She had someone coming to pick up an old baby toy that she had for sale on the internet, and they were at my front door to pick it up.

Being the best husband in the world, I stopped running and ran up two flights of stairs from the basement to our second story guest room to grab this toy, then back down one story and out the front door to deliver the toy to the person in the driveway paying 5 dollars for it. Once the hand off was made I smiled at the stranger and raced back into the house. I flew down the flight of stairs to the basement where I hopped back on the treadmill. I didn't stop running during this whole process. It irritated me to divert from my task that was so close to completion. Once I got back into the basement and back on the treadmill, it only took seconds before my knee felt a familiar pain. Damnit!

I was in disbelief. No flipping way was this happening right now! I was pissed to say the least but part of me was confused because the pain in my knee was familiar, but this time it was the other knee. The same pain. The exact same pain. Just the other knee. I knew what I was in for but didn't want to accept the truth. I finished my run and got off the treadmill. I knew what to do. I needed to stretch it out, right? I learned that trick from having the same thing happen to my other knee just a little over one year ago. I needed to stretch. I also knew how to deal with the pain. It sucked but that was okay. I was enjoying the suck of life. How could things get any worse? I really didn't care. I just wanted to run. "Why am I injury prone?", I asked myself. I continued to doubt my capability and wondered, "Is it genetics? Am I just not meant to run?" I didn't want to give myself the opportunity for an excuse and got to work trying to stop the pain before it got worse.

The next few days I tried to run more and more but made sure I stretched before and after my runs. It didn't make a difference. I could still only run about a half of a mile before the pain set in, but I would force myself to run at least two miles before calling it. I knew nothing was broken so I tried to see how far I could take this pain. Maybe my knee would fix itself or just finally give in and snap so I could have an answer to what the hell was wrong with my knee.

I kept pushing past the pain until one day I tried to run three miles, and by mile two the pain was so unbearable I couldn't run anymore or for that matter walk. I hobbled a mile home in excruciating pain. I decided to go seek medical help right then and there. I wanted to heal faster than the last time. I wasn't discouraged. I was driven to overcome my problem. There was no running from this, literally.

Does opportunity have a rope

I felt defeated once again. I was back in my hole of self-pity. I didn't quit though. I knew I needed to fix the problem and keep falling forward. I didn't want to go see a real doctor, so I went and had acupuncture done for a few weeks. I had been trying my stretching routine for a couple months with acupuncture added to the mix and there was no change with my knee. The pain would come and go like a bolt of lightning out of nowhere but especially prominent if I tried to run any kind of distance. When all of that didn't fix anything, I went to see a sports medicine doctor to see if that would be any different.

Once I sought help from a sports medicine doctor and discussed my issue with him, he too was baffled. I didn't tear anything. Nothing was broken. Hence why I didn't go to the Emergency Room. I probably should have gone to see an Orthopedic surgeon. It may have been cheaper in the long run instead of paying for all the sessions I was going through. I sure was glad to be employed again so I could pay for all this help.

I will say, the sports doc was confident he could figure out my issue and get me back to running. Long story short and a few hundred dollars later, he hits on my problem. It was a nerve being compressed in my lower back. I'm telling you as soon as he hit the problem area in my lower back, the pain was gone. I was impressed but also baffled. I shuffled around for a couple weeks after that last appointment dreading the pain would return with fury. It never did.

Even though I wasn't running and avoiding anything intensive to my back and legs, I still went crazy on the spin bike which didn't cause me any residual pain because it wasn't compressing the nerves in my back. I also did a little weightlifting on my arms and upper body. I needed to keep my guns looking ripped.

Besides working out during my free time, I was also in the process of studying to take some certification exams for career growth and to broaden my skill set in certain areas. I had work to do. Progress doesn't stop. Just because you're handicapped in one area doesn't mean you're a complete loss. You are still capable of accomplishing goals, right?

I studied a lot in that time of dealing with my knee injury and ended up taking some exams. I failed them all. I felt stupid. Absolutely stupid. Not only was I in shit pain but I also felt like I had a brain full of mush. I'm pretty good at digging myself into a hole but I remembered I can't give up.

Was I really digging myself deeper into my hole or was I trying to climb out of it? I knew what it felt like to be in that hole of defeat but if I looked at it from another angle, I knew I could get myself out of it.

I remembered that the greatest tool in the Devil's toolkit is discouragement. When he cannot conquer you with every other tool he has, he throws that at you. Well, screw that noise. I'm not a quitter. I took most of those exams again and passed them. A few hundred dollars later and I had restored faith in myself. Take your discouragement and shove it up your ass Satan. Not today! I got shit to do.

I will say, if you're not careful or aware of your situation and don't realize the hold that your emotions have on you, you can easily stay in the hole you're in. If you've never experienced sadness or discouragement in your life, you're a liar. As I stated before, sadness is that funk that you just can't get out of sometimes. It can feel like your legs are stuck in the muck and mire. You just can't pull yourself out of it.

I like to compare sadness to the other medical terms like depression or people who are manic or whatever. But the truth is, sadness is your own little pity party. We like to think that we're better than we really are and when things don't work out, we throw a great big old pity party of sadness for ourselves. Again, our expectations are too high and when we get let down, we turn to feeling sorry for ourselves.

I understand a lot of us are wired to run when things don't work out. We run and crawl in a hole to console ourselves. It's the fight or flight response. I am fully capable of doing the same thing by running away from difficult situations. In a way, it's quitting.

There are times when I ask myself, "Why do I always screw everything up?" That question right there puts me into that hole. I wallow around in that hole feeling sorry for myself like I haven't accomplished anything in my life. Which I know is a lie. It's hard to see otherwise. No one can talk you out of it either. Once you're convinced you are the most worthless piece of crap on planet Earth, you'll become sunk in the funk.

My advice to combat landing in that hole is to simply, not believe it. It's a lie and you shouldn't lie to yourself to make you feel worse. Accept the situation and forgive yourself for getting to that point. You need to carry on with the belief that you are capable of accomplishing anything. We all fail. Get over it. Move past it because it is in the past.

I've said it many times in this book but if you're going to fail, fall forward. Pick yourself up off the ground and take a step forward.

Another way of getting over self-doubt is to reflect back to something you did right. Our past can help us overcome the present, most of the time.

Let's take an example of how I handled taking certification exams to be able to distinguish myself and have credibility in my industry. The exams I take are a couple hundred dollars each. It's not cheap to fail an exam. When I fail an exam, I don't accept my failure and give up. No, I have failed many tests before. I know I have to retake them ASAP and give it my all. Sometimes money limits how many times I can retake the exams, but I still don't let that discourage me. I let my past failures remind me that I have passed a few certifications by sticking to my studying routine and taking the exams again.

If you feel like you're a failure, try to find an instance in your past that relates to your current situation. Find motivation from it and conquer what's troubling you.

What's hard to realize is that sadness usually comes from some other emotions, right? Sometimes we're so happy and so excited about something and all of a sudden, sadness creeps in. Why? Because we got our hopes and dreams crushed. We set the bar too high.

What I have understood while dealing with sadness during times in my life is that you have to suck it up and get over it. Things don't work out like we want them to every time. There's no point in throwing a pity party. Everyone fails a few times in their life if not thousands of times.

You have to pick yourself up, dust yourself off and smack defeat square in its face and say, "I am not a worthless piece of shit. I will conquer this uphill battle." Thrust yourself forward into the flames of the battle you're in. There is no point in throwing a pity party over things out of your control. The only thing to do is to go hard and be humble in your failures.

Can I stand on opportunities shoulders

What if your sadness comes from not feeling like you are as accomplished as others? You fail while others succeed. Don't compare yourself with other people.

Accept that there are people out there that are better than you. Maybe you are just not as good as you think you are. Next time tell yourself that you are as good as you are right now and that you will be better in time.

There are people in this world that are better than you. That's a fact. Once you understand that, then you can understand how to get over the emotion of sadness creeping in your life because things didn't go your way. There is always somebody better than you or somebody in a worse situation than you're in. If you can realize that, you can realize that there's no point in being sad or discouraged about anything in your life.

Take yourself out of the equation when being depressed, sad, or feeling sorry for yourself. Thinking of yourself in those times may lead to you doing something to punish yourself for being what you think you are. Just realize you may not know who you are yet, but also understand that you are not Billy Bob or Bobby Sue from Beltwater (those are not real people and I'm not sure that's a real town). You are you and don't give up because you didn't meet your expectation of yourself that you created by comparing yourself to someone else. It's okay to be you. It's okay to fail. It's okay to be different. This world takes all kinds and that means you too.

One thing that may help you turn a competitive or high expectation situation on its head is to kill your ego and let the competition do the work for you. Don't let your ego get in the way of the vision or perception of yourself. If there is a win-win between you and someone else, take it. Especially if they are doing all the work and getting most of the glory. Just by being included in their work, you will obtain a share in the profits. There's no point in competing in a losing situation when you can find a way to take the high road and still stay on top. That's being a leader!

I know a lot of people go through those times of doubt in their lives. You may feel as though you are not as good as such and such because they are always perceived as being right by everyone around you. You are always the one who has to play as the inferior who's not worthy of ever knowing any valuable information. I went through it before. Serving other people from an inferior perspective. It's called a job!

No matter if you're a leader or the lowest person in the org chart, you have to play as part of the team. Just like the role of a host at a party, you have to make everyone feel welcomed and important. You are performing the role of an inferior. This life isn't about keeping up with the Jones'. It's about being relevant and contributing what you can with what talents you have.

What makes you special? How can you help other people with your talents? What do you have to contribute for the benefit of others?

Don't get caught up in what other people's talents are or what you may believe they perceive you as. It can be a nasty place to feel like you're always being judged. To live a life based on what other people think of you and what you're capable of, is a dark life. Just know there is more common ground between you and the rest of the world than there is uncommon ground.

The key is to point out our similarities instead of our differences during times of disagreement or discouragement. If the other party is unwilling to reason, you have to keep your head held high and know you are vindicated even if no one else can see it. Let them win and take what is given to you. That's a real win-win.

Ever heard the phrase, "Any publicity is good publicity." If you're causing ripples in the water, then you are on someone's mind. The brain can play tons of games with you, I know. Life in general is a game where no one wins. Try not to dwell on the insignificant. Especially if you're trying to size up someone else's perception of you.

When I run, I run just to get those thoughts out of my head. Thoughts like; What Nancy thinks of my shoes, if I sounded dumb in some conversation, or whatever the fuck else I felt odd about in my day. I need to run to keep falling forward and leave all the bullshit behind me. I have to get out to run so I can get that pile of doubt out of my head. I have to tell myself I cannot believe my suspicions and not fall into the snare of depression from discouragement. Over and over I have had to tell myself that **I AM** an awesome SOB. In those times, you know, if it wasn't for running, I'm pretty sure I would still be in a ditch trying to dig my way out.

Running was my way out. It is my escape. Even if it is painful and sucks. Although, at this point in time of my life, running was diminishing due to injury. I was running out of options to deal with life. I didn't have many win-win situations popping up. I had to do something. My usual avenues of release were not working. What was I going to do? How would I deal with all the perceptions and paranoia of what everyone thought of me? I didn't have a way, or the time, to process all my interactions from the day.

Usually the time during my run helped me to convince myself that no one was actually out to get me. I may be paranoid. I may have anxiety. I can see that now.

I'd get hung up on what other people are thinking; "Are they thinking about me?", "Are they intentionally trying to deceive me?", "Are they fucking with me or being serious?" Without running, how was I going to clear my head of all that bullshit?

The reality is that most people are not out to get you or care about your life. It's really unlikely that someone is intentionally out to get you or do you harm. The majority of the time they are thinking about themselves and what they can do to make them look more important. I realize that now but at the time, I was judging myself and my actions with severe prejudice.

Even when I was a young adult, I really started to lean on how people viewed me. Maybe it was because I always watched what other people did and judged them. It's possible? Regardless of the reason, I took more consideration into what people thought about me as a person than what I thought of them. That then rolled into what I thought about myself. That process turned into mental warfare with myself. I had to scream at myself, "Stop thinking of what other people think of you!"

I think I was caught up in what people thought of me because of what I had thought of them. If I had an opinion of them then surely, they thought something about me. After coming to terms with my perception or paranoia, I realized that not everyone on this planet is going to like me and there is nothing I can do to change that. Tell me, do you like everyone you come into contact with? If you say yes, you're a liar.

We like people because we have something in common with them. If we find that there are no similarities then we don't care to interact with them, right? If we are forced to interact with people we do not care for, there is usually an awkward conversation about the weather involved, right?

The fact remains that you won't be liked by some people, and you may not like some of them as well. That's how it is. We can't always see eye to eye. There will always be haters, but you need them to keep yourself in check. They will help to validate who you are and who you are not. Don't get caught up in their opinion because they are just that, opinions! That's not who you really are but damnit if you don't know who you are, then you need to do some searching to figure that out.

It may take some time to realize who you are. You may not like what you find out about yourself but at least you have the potential to be what you want to be, in time. We evolve over time and change into our perceived selves. Who you are today may not be who you are tomorrow.

When I was unemployed and searching for a new job, I didn't know who I was. I questioned every single ounce of me. I questioned who I was and what I stood for, what I believed in and what I was capable of. There's nothing more conflicting than constantly beating yourself up for not living up to your standard, or someone else's. That conflict will leave you in a funk of disablement that will make you feel like you don't want to live anymore and contemplate suicide or come up with crazy workout routines that are ignorant and may lead to jacking up your knee.

You must fight to ignore the deceit that your mind is playing on you. You have the right to live and to be as free as every other person on this Earth. You are just as good, if not better, than the majority of everyone else on this planet. You are worth the breath that you take. Know it. Believe it. Convey it.

Is it opportunity or is it just me

One place that can lead to the spread of the misconception about yourself is the Internet. Social media is proof that you can be controlled by others, emotionally. Be careful not to fall into the snares of the Internet trolls out there. It can make you believe other people's opinions about you are real, instead of you knowing who you are. It makes you soft. It makes you weak and vulnerable to be controlled by someone's out of context words. Our society has become less of a real deal America who's tough and confident, and turned it into something that's more of a socially awkward, emotionally distraught and soft culture. That is sickening.

It breaks my heart to see people being controlled by what other people think about them. I've heard of people committing suicide because of it. You see it on the news. It's a real threat. People commit suicide because they are fed up with how people talk about them. Their character has been diminished into nothing. It's all thanks to the multiple ways to slander someone on the Internet. Social media can ruin people's lives. It can crumble them with one person telling the truth, or maybe lying about it, who knows. The fact of the matter is, that's the power of social media. It's able to feed you so much information that you don't have time to dissect it. All you can do is dissect and judge yourself. Why put yourself on par with what other people are doing?

Think about those individuals that go on mass killing sprees. What influence do you think the Internet and social media had on them? I'm sure all the information overload and misconceptions on social media has driven them to conceive themselves as something they are not. Media, social or not, does a great job of feeding us bullshit to the point that we believe we are something we are not.

My hope is that we can all start to realize this truth and not allow us to make poor decisions that hurt us or others. At one point we used the Internet as a way to escape from the real world. Today we use the real world to escape from the Internet.

In all sincerity, who cares what other people are doing. There are people out there that are better than you, different from you and similar to you. There's a lot of things that I can't do but other people can do. I don't care. I'm going to do whatever I know I can do and make friends with all those that are the same as me. If I can't do something but want to, I'm going to bust my ass to figure out how to do it.

I will be sure to solicit advice from those that are better than me because they may have done what I'm trying to accomplish. I'm competitive but I don't give up and accept the fact that I'm a loser or I'll never be good at anything because social media tells me that. You cannot believe everything on social media and the Internet.

Take some time to enjoy solitude or time away from technology so you can find yourself and figure out who you are and what you're made of. Clear your mind of its clutter and come back stronger. Go out and get physical to build your mental toughness.

Physical exertion points will test your mental ability. By overcoming those physical obstacles mentally, it will prepare you to be able to deal with real life conflicts. I'm telling you, there is a way that you'll be more focused in real world scenarios if you can just break through your own physical limitations, mentally. Social media cannot help you with this.

It's hard to exercise or test your physical limits if you're sitting in a chair surfing the web to validate your ego. We all need a break from technology sometimes so we can reconnect with ourselves. That break shouldn't include eating donuts and gossiping with friends. Doubt me? Go for a run. Do some push-ups. Try something different. Read a book. See for yourself what it can do for you, mentally.

I'm not a doctor. I don't have a Ph.D. I'm not a psychologist. This is my experience. When I am emotionally distraught, I go and try to hurt myself physically. Yes, I know that is probably not the best way to deal with what I'm going through, but it tests my mental capacity. I'm not actually trying to kill myself, but I do want to feel again when life becomes numb. I want the feeling of intensity. I want to know that I am alive, and I can make it through whatever obstacles are in my way. I tell myself, "I am a beast to be reckoned with." My mind is the only one that limits my physical abilities.

The only reason why I think this is true for me is because I know that if I can get over my mental limitations by running that extra mile or doing those extra sets in my workout, I can mentally overcome any emotional state I may be in. It takes mental toughness to run that extra mile and do those extra sets. I know that I'm mentally strong enough to not believe the doubt that I cast in my mind when I want to give up. Especially the doubt that comes with social media.

So, when you're feeling depressed and beating yourself up by believing that you're no good or that you're not made for this world and that nobody wants you around, go and do something about it. Every action has a reaction. If you don't act on it, nothing will change. Nothing. Changing nothing brings no change. You have to be the change. If you won't do it, no one else will. Get up, get after it and quit being lazy. Take initiative to do good for yourself.

This life is about you against you. You have to get over you! Who cares what anybody else thinks? What everybody else thinks isn't really what you think? That's outside influence and that shit doesn't matter. You want to be confident? You don't want to be depressed? Then quit feeling sorry for yourself. Go and do something about it that will make you proud of yourself. Forgive yourself for letting it happen but more importantly, don't give up. Get after it and get it done.

When you start to feel yourself being low, you need to lift yourself up because no one is going to do it for you. Act quickly and don't stay down too long. You have to be that deciding factor. You have to dig deep and tell yourself not to give up. Screw everyone else. They can go eat a big bag of bricks. Yeah that's the hard truth of dealing with emotions. You have to deal with them! No one else, but you!

So, when dealing with these emotions, choose to go on the high road. Deal with it however you have to deal with it. Get mad. Go lift weights. Go run your anger out. Run it out.

I don't care how bad it hurts to deal with your emotions or what it makes you think of yourself. You have to deal with it in a way that ultimately puts your own perception of yourself into a positive light. Purge yourself of all the negativity that you've built up inside of you. Let your light shine. Be the real you, without excuses. Be authentic.

What you need to focus on is being better than you were yesterday. That's the God honest truth. If we're not learning about ourselves, we're not moving forward. Continuous learning and progress are the only way that we can keep our minds sharp, focused and not stuck in a hole. When we're not being productive, we're sitting around feeling sorry for ourselves for what we did or didn't do at some given point in time.

Just thinking about sadness makes me angry. I feel pissed off when I start feeling sad for myself. And that pissed off feeling gets me motivated to go out and try to go hard and put in the time so I can feel happy about who I am. Because isn't that what we all want? We all want to be happy with ourselves!

We don't want to be people who are just pissed off all the time or people who are always sad and feeling sorry for themselves and feeling worthless. Although on the flip side, I definitely don't care to be one of those people who are so filled with hope that they are blind to reality. It is sickening how delusional they are. Ugh.

I get it. We can't be happy all the time. Though all we want is to be happy. We just want to love and be loved. If you don't take away anything else from this book, just know and realize that life is life. You have to go through it. Be satisfied with what you have. Feel satisfaction and be at ease with what is going on in your life. Don't chase after the wrong priorities to try to satisfy that big hole in you. Let your hole finally feel whole.

Part Five:

In the End

Chapter 10

Taking the High Road

Most times in my life, and especially during the writing of this book, I have always depended on what everyone else thought about me, but especially what I looked like. Though, while writing this book, and laying all my feelings down on paper for you to scowl over, I have become free from myself and outside influence. I won't be arrogant and say I'm now impervious to influence or rejection. No I am not, but I am more aware of it. Being aware of your emotional state and understanding how easily we can be influenced or nudged into thinking a certain way, can lead you to being confident in your assertions.

My whole goal with this book has been to help guide you through thought processes to go through when you start to feel your emotions bubbling up out of control. I always want you to keep yourself in check. Don't let yourself become so flush with passion that it washes you down through the gutters of life. You should be able to climb the hill of defeat and take the road to greatness by understanding how and when to react to situations that may not fall in your favor.

Take your time and be patient when responding or reacting to others. Keep their feelings in mind. Treat them as your superior because at the end of the day we are meant to serve others with unconditional love and compassion.

You have to be somewhat emotionally available but also be aware of what the outcome may be if you let your emotions take over. Keep a rational head. Understand your feelings and understand what goes through your mind when you're in that state of emotion. You may have to walk away from situations and that's okay. It's better to save face than to regret what you may say or do.

I hope some of these tips and tricks that you've read about, can help prepare you to overcome obstacles in your daily life. Whether that's being able to run a 5k, 10K, a marathon, or to be able to get over your fears of something completely different, like talking to that crush you've had your eye on. Use this newfound knowledge to your advantage.

You are a lot more capable than you believe you are. It's only through your choice of action and devotion to change yourself for the better that will ultimately make you a better person. You have to strive for excellence and not beat yourself up over your failures. We all fail but that's how we learn to win.

It's very important to be humble when you do win. Just because you've won doesn't give you the right to shove it in people's faces. You have to take the high road and be humble. When you start acting humble you start to build mental strength around outcomes in your life. Life sucks but you have to be able to navigate it and you need a strong mind to navigate it with. Those that have weak minds will never last long nor will they ever accomplish much. You have to be strong mentally to become strong physically, but you may have to go through something physically to become stronger mentally.

I've laid out some tools that I have found that have gotten me through tough times, and good times. These tools and those things that I've learned have made me a better person. But mostly they have made me aware of who I am and how I can get when faced with obstacles in my life. Maybe I can get through this life and make my reality a little more comfortable knowing what I know now. Even if every day I try to find comfort in being uncomfortable because that's what drives me to keep falling forward. The struggle and suffering keeps me moving on.

Where do you find strength

It is me against myself against the world and the only tools I have at hand are my courage, discipline, and faith in God. I'll give all glory to God with His power and mercy that He has bestowed on me. With His knowledge and through His will, anything is possible.

You are capable of all things too but first you need to believe in yourself. Also trust that others believe in you. When you feel like no one else believes in you, trust that someone out there in fact does believe in your abilities.

You have to know that some other human being out there believes in you. I believe in you! Just because you don't know me, and I don't know you doesn't mean I can't believe in your abilities. I am a trusting person and will always give someone the benefit of the doubt before making a decision on if you're fully capable or not. There are a lot of beings out there with untapped talents. They're just scared to use them or don't know they have them.

I believe we all have potential in us that has yet to be tapped. Dig deep and find that well of life down inside you. It's there. You have to bring it to the surface. No one else can do it for you. You can be shown the way but ultimately you have to make the first move. Do it before time runs out because it will run out. We all have an expiration date. We just don't know when it is.

Death will come for you but that doesn't mean that you should be scared of it. Nor should you be happy for death to come. That's not the point of life. The purpose of life is to find out who you are. Understand that death comes for us all but in this race that we call life, there is no finish line. You will leave things undone. You will never be finished searching for who you are either. We change over time and may have to rediscover ourselves if we happen to lose touch with who we thought we were. Just know that you will never be done fighting. You will have to find new ways of adapting to everyday life by finding those talents you've stored away. If you suffer long enough, they will come into light.

You will always have something to overcome. Another obstacle. Another metal to achieve. Another mile to run. Embrace the challenge. Go full force towards it and see what you're made of. Wake up and be grateful for another day, another breath or another second with the ones you love. Don't squander away your untapped potential because you're afraid of your own emotions. Put yourself in check and realize your emotions are just a recommendation of how you should be presenting your feelings to the world. Be stronger than your thoughts.

You have to have emotional intelligence these days just to survive in this jacked up world we've created. If you cannot control your emotions, they will control you.

Think about that phrase "If you cannot control your emotions, they will control you". You could interpret that in two different ways depending on your perception. The first meaning could state that if you cannot control your emotions, the emotion will do all your decision making for you in that moment. On the other hand, "they will control you" could mean an actual person. It's there to indicate a power that's outside of your control. People are fully capable of preying on others and their emotions. Not all abuse is physical.

What kind of signal do you think you send to others when you act irrationally over a situation? Do you think they could take notice of how upset something they said or did made you? Could they use that information to their advantage down the road? Have you ever had someone push your buttons or make you feel bad about yourself just by saying a few words to you? Once they hijack your emotional responses, they will have control over you and your reactions. It can become a game for them where they find enjoyment in fucking with you.

You may be baited into acting out just so they can pin something against you later. If you can control your emotions, you can control your reactions to people and situations in the most critical of times. You have to become an emotional master.

How is this possible

Emotional masters are all around us. Think about Actors. They're people who have complete control and manipulation of their emotions while acting. Their job is to project specific emotions when called upon while performing on the stage. They can project happiness, fear, anger and more. Some can even shed a tear at the drop of a hat. Wow.

Yes, that is an impressive talent but how many of them do you think really have control over their emotions when it comes to off screen reality? Some may project it well while off screen, but do they really feel that way? I don't know any superstar actors personally, but I can tell you by watching the news about some of them, that we really don't know them. Some of their closest people may not know them either. That may be because they are so great at disguising their emotions. If Actors and Actresses are only faking it for your enjoyment on screen, I truly hope they do not continue their disingenuous actions off screen.

Even for a moment, if you have to lie to save face or pretend to be nice, I don't really agree with it. Acting, in the real world, just to make it through life, is not genuine. You should be truthful and honest no matter the outcome. If you don't, it will drive you insane. You could possibly do harm to yourself because of the damage you've done by lying to yourself about who you are in the real world. Once the truth sets in, you'll be in for a rude awakening.

Take any of the famous people that you have seen on the news in the past years who have taken their own life. What do they say about them? "Oh, they were such a great and outgoing person. I never saw it coming." Yep. But that goes to show that just because someone who can manipulate their emotions so well, still have not become emotional masters. Suicide is giving in to the emotional distress and discouragement of life. I can fully understand the reasoning why someone would do that because I've been there. Hell, I'm still trying to climb out of that hole. I may be on the high road, but I'm stuck in the ditch holding a tow strap waiting for a snatch out of the mud.

Emotional Masters, like Actors, are artists of emotional competence. There is nothing they cannot convey. Regardless of if they believe it to be true or not. They are the best "fakers" on Earth. Don't take that the wrong way though. It's meant to be a compliment to those who are the best at emotional manipulation.

Think about those who cannot act as well or are not liked as much and ousted for being fake. Huh what? If you're not fake enough, you're called out for being fake?! Yup. I guess those who master their emotions can make anyone believe they are genuine.

In this life, I feel more like a comedian than anything else. I cannot act but I can act out. Comedians have a wonderful grasp on their emotions. They also know how to manipulate yours. Unlike actors they have one goal in mind. To make you laugh. I regard comedians as very smart people. They have a natural way of finding the fun in everything even when times may not be the best. They will lift up your spirits but at the same time may be sacrificing themselves for your enjoyment.

How many comedians, especially in standup, do you think are really telling the truth during their bit even if it exposes their faults? I'm sure most all of them do but I do not know that for a fact. It seems as though they are willing to sacrifice their perception of themselves just to make you laugh. I can see why. Sometimes we all need to poke fun at our own faults so we can feel better about ourselves. It makes us human and it's a great way to heal our wounds or get over what we think about ourselves. You have to be able to laugh at your mistakes or shortcomings. By that I mean, you shouldn't take things so seriously but acknowledge where your faults lie. If you cannot do that then you're not being honest with yourself about who you really are. Try to humble yourself to the point where you can relax and have fun. Take a vacation some time so you can enjoy your own company.

Another example of emotional mastery is to look at professional athletes. They have to be rock solid and not allow their emotions to take control of them in clutch situations. They have to remain calm and "take it easy" while they do their job. Sure, they can have fun, but they have to do all of it while millions of people watch them live on TV or in person at the stadiums.

Imagine the players in championship games of baseball or football. Yes, they are ultimately just doing their job, but they have to be on point 100 percent of that game. They cannot lose their shit!

Though, some of them do and I know those who are watching, question that person's integrity. Integrity is a very important part of our character. We are judged by others for our status of integrity.

Those who are unsuccessful in controlling their emotions in tough times are destined to fail in the eyes of the onlookers. That's not to say they cannot be redeemed, because it can happen. It may be difficult and probably take more time than it should, but it isn't impossible.

A professional athlete cannot become unhinged no matter what. Win or lose. They have to keep it all buttoned up. That also goes for you and me. The nobody's of the world. We have to keep calm so our emotions can stay in check during our daily routines. If we don't, there will be consequences.

The consequence of not keeping it together can be minuscule but can also have a great effect on your life and what you think about yourself or how others perceive you. If you scream at someone because you didn't like what they said to you or did something you didn't agree with, don't you think there will be a consequence for your action? Now, given it might not be too severe but, it will impact you one way or another.

You may or may not speak to that person ever again, but I bet they might lock you up in that jail cell in their mind and never want anything to do with you again. You do not want to be in that jail. It's not worth fighting to get out once you're in there anyways. Avoid ending up there at all costs in the first place. Let the other person win if you have to. I'm sure all they want to do is feel important anyways.

We all want to feel important. Maybe we yell to prove our point to feel important in our interactions. I'm not saying bowing down to someone raising their voice is the right thing to do but it will save you a lot of emotional stress if you just let the words pass through you while you smile and nod your head.

When to be cautious

Being an Emotional Master isn't just about controlling how you react but also controlling what you say, when you say it and how you say it. What if you happen to unintentionally leak some sort of valuable information that could be of detriment to others or a place you're working at? No matter how comfortable you may feel around other people, do not gossip. Think before you speak. It could do more harm than you may understand at the time.

You never know how the other end is going to perceive your reactions. That person may be there to get that information out of you, but they may also be innocent and there to comfort you by listening. On the other hand they may decide they should use that information to better themselves. I mean it could happen. I'm paranoid at times. You don't know what anyone else is thinking nor can they know what you are thinking. The mind is unhackable from everyone on the outside of it.

So, when you start to feel something, whether it's a good emotion or a bad one, think before you speak. You could ruin your career or the career of your peers. One thing is for certain, don't intentionally be an asshole! If you know better and realize it's wrong before you move forward with your action, that's just plain evil. You will pay for it immediately or at a later time. Do good all the time no matter if someone is watching or not. Don't be a prick. Those who you notice that are that way and are intentionally out to do harm to people and their reputation, leave them be. They will get what's owed to them at some point. Find peace knowing that.

There are these types of people in this world that are all around us, they are deceitful beings. They will want to use your knowledge against you to better themselves and rid you from their life. The key is to not get so emotionally attached that you become blind to handing out information. These types of people string you along, for as long as they can, so they can continue to get information out of you to profit them as much as they can until throwing you to the waste side. I know people who have applied this technique before. They were intentionally deceitful because they were jealous of the other person and wanted what they had. Do not get hung up with jealousy or being envious.

Don't let people get into your head but if they do, realize it's just your mind working overtime trying to solve a problem it doesn't need to solve.

Ponder on this a little while. Do we create our thoughts or do our thoughts create us? That's a very deep and loaded question. It hits at the heart of all our problems. See the truth is, both questions have yes answers.

Yes, we do create our thoughts but if we end up obsessing over a thought for too long, we will start to believe the thought to be true. We project an idea to our mind and let it mull it over for a while until we like the outcome and believe it's in line with our morals. If we leave our thoughts to fester on a subject, it can eventually change us into something we are not. Depending on the emotional severity of the thought, it could cause us to change our morals or beliefs of reality in a negative manner.

Jealousy and envy is a great emotional example of this trap. Be careful with how long you debate with yourself on personal feelings over others. You could be so obsessed that you may act out of spite of someone or something and do something you'll regret later. Is that hate smoldering inside again?

Envy can destroy you and make you mad. Not mad as in angry but mad as in insane. You can lose all touch with reality while being hung up over so and so and what they did to you or what they have that you don't. Who gives a shit? Go do you. Take care of yourself and keep your nose out of their business.

If people feel the need to gossip about what they've been doing or what they just bought, listen but don't compare yourself to them. Gossip isn't always about oneself either. More frequently it's about what someone else did or what they have. Don't be jealous. Be happy for them. Show them love and acceptance. Make it a positive situation. Look them in their eyes, put your hand on their shoulder and tell them, "Bless your heart." Then walk away like you have something to do. More importantly, do it with a smile on your face. Smiling will give you so much more confidence in all that you do. Don't discount the power of a smile.

What you should do instead

What envy should really be driven by is the thought of having better relationships. It's okay to be envious of others' social abilities. Like how well of a conversationalist they are or how well they seem to make friends. If that envy drives you to get out of isolation so you can get out to talk to people to build better and long-lasting relationships, why wouldn't you want that type of envy? You get to choose your friends. Hopefully you will find commonalities and be just as happy with your relationships as everyone else.

Spending more time with those you love is priceless. That's real envy. Envious of time well spent. You don't realize what you should be envious of until you lose it. Relationships are so much more valuable than materialistic possessions. It is the source of the good and the bad. In the end, you will wish for more relationships and quality time with those you love.

Before you can build solid relationships, you have to learn to deal with your own problems and stay out of everyone else's. That's not to say that if you feel someone is in danger, or needs some lifting up, that you should ignore them and go on about your business. No, go out and help them. You may gain a deeper relationship with them.

Again, be compassionate and empathetic towards others. Build those relationships. Try to be happy and help others through the love of another human being. We are all on the same spaceship and it's been here for some time now. I think it's about time for us to realize that and start to get along with each other. We can only do that if we are comfortable with ourselves and drop all envious thoughts about everyone else. That's the understanding we need to grow between us all. The knowledge that you and I may be on separate paths but in the end, we are all going to the same destination.

Healthy relationships cannot be stabilized if you are shattered. You have to make sure you are whole if you want a solid foundation for your relationships. You have to heal your wounds and accept who you are first. The true process of healing is laying it all on the table. It's about exposing all of your truths about yourself just like a comedian might. Whether it's a past you don't want to bring up or something you're ashamed of. Healing is about being honest and open and not afraid of your past self. The only way to truly know yourself is to let other people know who you are. Especially those deep dark secrets you don't want anybody to know about. Healthy relationships are built on trust. That takes knowing someone and all that they are through their truths.

If you don't expose the darkness deep within you and let the light around you shine, you can never be whole. We all have light and darkness within us. It's just a matter of getting them in balance with each other.

Exposing ourselves and our faults are part of forgiving ourselves for who we believe we are. If you don't talk to someone or let others know how you feel, you will never accept yourself for who you truly are. Through the process of opening up to others, we can find similarities that we can relate to one another with. When that happens, you know you have been forgiven. If you can't accept yourself, how do you expect others to accept you for who you are?

Chapter 11

Keep Falling Forward

To this day I'm still the kid on the playground who sits by himself. I wait for people to walk up to me if they feel the urge to talk. I don't go out and seek relationships. I now realize that by doing that, I won't create many valuable relationships and will probably miss out on getting to know a lot of interesting people.

I'm okay with that. I like to keep my relationships to a minimum. I'd rather have more meaning behind my relationships instead of having human interaction to just have something to do. What's funny about that aspect of me is because in this part of my life, I had thrusted myself into a job that is based on how well you make relationships. You are judged on your interactions with people and how well they like you.

This is the same dream job that fell into my lap that I mentioned a couple chapters back. It happened to be that first rung of the ladder that helped me climb out of the hole I was in. The job's primary role was sales. Which means a ton of interaction with people. Most of them I've never met before in my life and may never meet again.

It's nerve rattling for me to be social in big groups but I do however enjoy striking up a one-on-one conversation with a complete stranger because you never know what you're about to get yourself into. It may lead to an unknown adventure through town or it may just be an interesting hour of your life. You'll never know unless you take that first leap to open up and genuinely act interested in the person next to you. Being curious is a great way to learn what you've never wanted to know.

I found out that in sales, you have to interact with everyone as if you've known them your whole life. You have to ask questions to get the other party to open up to you and believe you are there for their benefit. I am that guy. I care about other people's issues. For one, I get to help them solve an issue they're having and I'm a great problem solver. It's also a chance to hopefully make them happy. Helping people with issues so they feel important to someone else is a great way to build new relationships. People buy from people they like.

When to speak up

First thing I want to note is, I am so grateful to have had that job but also for the person who opened the opportunity up to me. Secondly, I believe it was the right job at the right time because I needed the challenge of being more sociable. I lacked that ability in my life, and I recognized that I needed to break out of my shell if I ever wanted to move forward.

Was I worried or scared? Yes! I was worried I wouldn't be able to exceed expectations like I had in the past with those more secluded technical roles. Usually, engineers are placed in the corner of the basement of some corporation and only get to come up to see the light of day when something breaks.

I was scared because I didn't like to be around a ton of people. One to four is a max for me. Anything over that I have to expel an exuberant amount of energy to keep up.

That aspect drags me down. As an introvert, I have to spend an equal amount of time in seclusion as I do socializing. If not more! It's all about balance. I can't do one without the other.

There is also the fact that to be good at that role in sales, I needed to be outgoing and talkative. I've never really been talkative, or for that matter outgoing. I'm a quiet and observant kind of man. Plus, I've always lived by a motto that I obtained as a young boy. "Speak only when spoken to" or "If you don't have anything valuable to contribute don't waste your breath".

When I was a little kid, my brothers used to tease me about what I would say. At the time I couldn't understand why but as an adult I completely understand and agree. I wasn't on the same page as them and couldn't speak in their terms. I was younger than them and didn't have anything to relate with them on, but I tried to interact anyway. I thought they were the coolest people on earth. I still do but back then I was too young to know how to be cool like them. I was just a kid in their eyes.

The reason why I am a quiet man is that I have been conditioned to feel like everything that comes out of my mouth is not going to be delivered well and I'll sound like the village idiot and be made fun of. I've had too many past experiences of failure to believe I'll be good at any of it today. I suck at speaking, but I also know if I feel horrible about what I said or how I may have come off, I am compelled to correct it. I don't care who you are. That part of me may never change. I don't like to talk but I have a compulsive issue to blurt out what I think is morally true no matter what the scenario may be. It's definitely a flaw.

I have to make it right and be clear on my intentions. I will not give in to defeat and accept the fact that I'm not perceived well, but rather do everything in my power to break the chain of social disablement. It's a work in progress. I usually make the situation more awkward than it already is by trying to clarify something I said. It always sounds better in my head but when it leaves my mouth, I usually instantly regret it. I really suck at communicating verbally.

Although recently, I've been able to practice that, the more I let go of caring about what people think about me, the more I'm able to open up and communicate effectively. I'm more careful on what I say and how I say things now, but I still feel that if I'm going to say something, it better add value. I'd rather be authentic in my presentation than do or say something just to fit in.

Being an introvert in an extrovert world is hard. That's a fact. It takes more effort to fake it than I care to put in, though I know it's not for my benefit but for the benefit of others. I can help a lot of people if I can open up and be outgoing. I have a lot to contribute.

Sometimes to counteract the drain of energy from social interaction, I tend to focus my attention on small tasks to complete. I don't have full awareness of my surroundings like I do when I'm in a smaller setting of people. Large groups make me uneasy, and I tend to lose my focus and get distracted by all that's going on around me. Most of the time it's too much for me to take in so I intentionally blur it out. It's a process that's been instilled into me for so long that it may take longer for me to reverse it.

Most of us have such thick calluses around who we believe we are that it's hard to change. If we do change, it takes a long time to be something other than what we are. It takes patience, persistence and perseverance to succeed. Once you get to the point of being changed, you've likely beaten yourself up so many times that you become as tough as steel.

How we evolve

I feel like my whole life has been similar to the process of creating Damascus steel. If you're not familiar with Damascus steel, it is a very hard piece of metal that has different metals forged together that are fired, beaten and cooled slowly. This process of bringing two different materials together to become one can be analogous to how we evolve as humans. We are constantly having to bring together an aspect that is foreign to us at the time but eventually it becomes who we are. It is an analogy that I can relate with to how I have been formed into the being I am today.

The process of forging is possible by intense heat and lack of oxygen. Just think of it as the process of running. When running, you're usually sweating due to overworking your muscles and also severely out of breath due to the lack of oxygen you can intake.

When faced with intense situations we become unable to breathe, we tend to take longer to cool or relax but eventually become harder or more knowledgeable than we were before. Just like running, it may suck while you're in the process of doing it but once you're done and have cooled down, you become stronger and more resilient to fatigue for future workouts. Whatever that process may be, whether it's running or learning a new language, we all get molded in this manner. Your toughness depends on what you've been able to suffer through.

It could be the process of a life of anguish and how much mental capacity you have had to exert to withstand the forces being pressed upon you, but somehow you still keep moving forward with life. It could be the process of a life lived with challenges that take you past your physical capacity. Some of this may be self-inflicted or delivered to you by external forces in your life that you have no control over.

You're heated, beaten, and molded by actions of your own, or by other people's actions towards you, but eventually you will find relief and become something so beautiful that other people will appreciate and desire to be like. The end result will always bring positivity. Perceive it as a good thing. If you can survive every challenge put forth upon you, you may become one of the hardest SOBs on planet Earth.

Once you've been hardened and shaped into what you are, there is still another step you must take. You have to go through the process of becoming as sharp as the blade that Damascus steel can produce. The reflection of your past is how you can understand what molded you, but this process of reflection will also allow you to sharpen your perspective of the world. Which ultimately makes you smarter or in this analogy, sharper.

Your blade of mental and physical readiness can become sharpened so much so that you can pierce like none other because of how well you were formed and honed. Your life experiences are the wet stone to sharpen your blade. You go through these processes of being thrown into the fire with objects that are foreign to you, beaten on and pummeled together until you come out on the other side feeling the well-deserved relief that can only come with growth and understanding that takes to change. What you can take away from those experiences and processes, whether they were good or bad, is that those are wins. You have come out on top if you make it through the process of change. We are always being tested and molded by fire.

Remember those trials, because that is what you can call upon the next time you get thrown into the fire. You can recall that you've overcome those obstacles and that you can overcome similar obstacles in your path. Recall your past and you will have the drive to never give up on any challenge you face. You will never quit because you know the outcome is something beautiful. It was meant to happen. You have to suffer through it before you find relief and begin the process of recovery.

You don't have to go through a hard life to be as hard as Damascus steel. You can put yourself into the fire and beat yourself up until you've accomplished your goal. I don't mean physically either but if you're into that thing, you can do that too. To each their own. But in that same sense, what I mean is that if you want to do something, or if you have a goal set out to accomplish, throw yourself into the fire. If you fail, have the strength to try again with the knowledge you gained from the last time. Take the leap of faith and trust you will gain something from the experience.

The method to build up grit to sharpen your blade is to get after it and fall forward towards that goal. Just fall forward into it! Next is to do whatever you have to do to accomplish that goal regardless of how many times you fail and fall down. Get back up until it's finished. Move forward!

Lastly, you have to give yourself the time to cool off and reflect back on what it took to get over that roadblock. Do that by noting your accomplishments. However big or small that goal was, remember you accomplished it. You did not quit. Your blade is now sharper than it was before. Your emotions and the control over your emotions should be trained in the same manner. It takes time but with mindfulness and patience, it can be achieved.

What else is there

On top of awareness of ourselves and being in control of our emotions, we have to believe. Whether that's faith in yourself or belief in God's power working within you. We can overcome emotional or physical obstacles by being so overly positive to a point that you have no other choice than to believe it will turn out okay. That to me, is the strongest of human powers. Being positive when there is no light. Having the will to be steadfast in those times of despair.

I believe wholeheartedly that our belief system is a direct result of our emotional stability. If you don't believe in yourself or believe that God can help you through whatever you may be going through, then you will fail, indefinitely. Through the process of positive thinking and our belief system, any emotion like anger, fear, greed, jealousy and sadness can all be overcome. When you find yourself in the midst of; anger, fear or sadness, just be aware of it and tell yourself you are not in the right state of mind to be making decisions. Maybe you need to look at yourself from an external perspective really quick and see if you're being negative. Step away and check yourself. You may need to change your attitude or perception before you can be of value, instead of being harmful.

You don't have to pray to God for change but that would be a good place to start for some. You can pray for yourself to get you through some difficult obstacle, and it will change your mind. Your mind will repent in a way. Forgive yourself for not trying hard enough. Pray for strength.

Emotions can be controlled through practice and disciplined awareness of yourself, and others, but you have to be strong. Strong in your faith. Strong in the belief of yourself.

Anybody who's ever overcome large obstacles in their lives will most likely attribute that to their faith in God. Just listen to some of the professional athletes while they're getting interviewed after winning a big game. Do you think they believe they accomplished that feat by themselves? No, they call upon all the powers within them and all the powers around them. Whether they give credit to God or the rest of the team, they believe it wouldn't have been possible without their belief in external powers.

God and prayer may be the most powerful energy on Earth. And with them you can overcome anything. Especially the emotional peril that we seem to all go through in our darkest of hours.

If you give prayer a shot, you will start to understand what that alone time in prayer can do for you. You may be saying "Prayer? I don't know how to pray. Why should I pray?" The simple answer to that statement is go find somewhere quiet for thirty minutes or so, close your eyes and be still. Let whatever goes through your head seep out of your ears. Let the little voice in your head ramble until it shuts up. You will find strength in that solitude. You may have to do that process every day for a couple weeks before that voice actually shuts up but eventually it will. Trust the process and "just be". You can resolve a ton of your issues if you give yourself time to clear them from your head.

I've been through some of the darkest hours of my life and made it to the other side, thanks to prayer. That alone time to reflect back on my past, or any other issue I was facing, helped me to be able to forgive myself for what I have done and to remind myself to let go of the small stuff. This life isn't guaranteed. You should be happy with what you have or don't have. Be happy just being.

We are all lucky to even exist together. This life is by chance because of a series of events that happened to bring it all together. Whatever made us is a powerful force we should all acknowledge and be thankful for that.

How change brings change

With this new outlook and perception, I have gained in my life, thus far, I started to view everything differently. I viewed my new role in sales as a learning experience and not just that, but one that could make me better than who I was yesterday. I understood that I needed to stop stressing out about not living up to everyone's expectations of me and start to respect myself for who I was and what I knew I was capable of. I also looked at running differently too.

While I was in the process of learning how to become more sociable and a better communicator, I started to feel more positive about myself. That positivity gave me a way to keep motivating and bettering myself. I had been injury free for a few months after the trip to the sports doc and was really wanting to run with this new motivation. Although I was continuously working out, I started to feel like I needed to change up my workout routine. I was getting bored and my legs were getting skinny. I had hit a plateau. So, why not attempt running again? The only thing that could go wrong is that I would hurt myself and not be able to run for a while. Why not give it a go?

I've said this many times before, but I hate running. I have never enjoyed it. Yes, there were times where it gave me peace and a place in time to clear my thoughts, but I never really wanted to go for a run. That's because I wasn't comfortable running.

When I started back running, and during my first few runs, I was contemplating how I was running. I'd question why I was running the way I was. I could never keep the same pace and always felt like my feet were slapping the ground funky and all that crap. So, one of the days while trying to get back into running, after being injury free for a couple months, I reflected on what I thought about while I ran and even what my expectation was of the run before I began my run. I figured out that I set myself up for failure before I even started running. My brain was getting in the way of my success.

Every time I planned my run, I knew how many miles I wanted to run and how long it should take me to finish. I even knew what route I would take that day. This set the bar for what I thought I needed to accomplish during that run so I could view it as successful.

I was stressed while running because I was focused on what my time was per mile, how high my heart rate was, and if I would make it to the end of the run without walking. None of that shit really matters if you just want to go for a run. Well, it kind of does if you're training for a long-distance race but the principle is still the same. Quit giving yourself limits and just run!

After realizing what I was doing to myself during my runs by over-thinking where I needed to run or how my stride should be or how fast I should be moving, I decided I would put this new theory of running free of rules into motion.

At this point I had only ran a handful of times since being injury free and most runs were only 3 miles long. My best times were ten plus minute miles. Not really fast but great if you are planning to run for a longer distance. My methodology for this experiment was simple, lace up my shoes and head into a certain direction. I knew I had an hour to run and whatever mileage I put in during that time was okay with me. For the most part I was just happy to be injury free and pain free. So I ran.

I didn't run at a certain pace. I didn't tell myself I needed to run slow to begin with and then crank it up for my next few miles so it would make the next mile a faster time than my first mile. No. I also wasn't concerned with how long I was going to run for. I let go of all that crap and just ran. I didn't care which route I took and planned for a longer than anticipated run each time I went out. Who knows what I would run into on my adventure? What if I ran into an alien life form? I'd have to stop and at least ask a couple of questions about the universe before I got back to my run.

Once I was able to truly run, I wasn't focused on how I was running. I simply ran at a pace that felt comfortable to me. That pace happened to be a 7:45 minute mile pace. That's fast for me. But I definitely could not keep that pace up. Oh hell no. I had to allow myself to walk a lot. I walked a lot to begin with, but I also didn't judge myself for walking.

With this new method of only running in a style that was comfortable, and then walking when I couldn't breathe or run properly, I was able to still maintain a decent pace of ten minute miles. Not too shabby for someone who would walk a lot and run a little. By running harder and faster, it worked my legs more and made my legs uncomfortably sore the next day. I liked that. More importantly, this method was making my legs stronger for the next round. I was throwing myself into the fire and reshaping my form.

With my old method of running, I viewed it as if I didn't run the entire time, then I wasn't running. If I had to walk, then I wasn't good enough. Well, I believe that's some bullshit. I started to view running as similar to lifting weights. When you lift weights, you don't hold the weights the entire time and only put them down when you're done with your workout, do you? No, you take breaks. Why was I not doing the same with running?

When lifting weights, you should also put your form before how much you lift. Form is very important to reducing injury. Who cares how little weight you are lifting as long as you can lift it properly? Same is true for running. If you are not running comfortably, you may be using the wrong form and will likely hurt yourself, like I have done so many times previously. Maybe that's why I hated running so much?

During my runs, and after understanding how much I should just run and forget all the shit I knew about running, I found myself looking forward to going running. So much so that I was cheerfully telling everyone I passed while I was out for a run, "Good Morning!" or "Hello!". I was all smiles. I'm pretty sure they probably thought I was weird but at least they smiled and responded back positively. You never know, maybe they will go on and achieve greatness from that act of kindness I showed.

Why you should just let go

I ran and walked and ran and walked. I did walk a lot but when I ran, I ran. I felt GREAT! I was experiencing real happiness and joy in running. It didn't suck as much anymore. I ended up running more miles than I thought I was capable of, or thought I would ever accomplish for that day, and eventually walked less each time I went out. That balance of running and walking had made my runs easier and more enjoyable. The process of smiling when I ran also had a great deal of impact on my attitude towards the run. I actually looked forward to running now. Ain't that something?

I no longer had the love hate relationship to running once I figured out how to attack my enemy using the method of not giving a shit. I have since then been running in this manner, carefree. Whatever happened would happen. I had no expectation of what I should be accomplishing as long as I put forth the effort to finish. It's also changed my perspective on things outside of running. I questioned what else in my life I haven't been viewing properly. What other things in my life could I perceive differently?

Once I was able to let go of all my concerns and just be present, I was now happier in those moments, and also managed the outcome better.

I quit caring. Though this is a different type of not caring. It's not one that has given up on life and all that is in it.

No. It's one that liberates you from all the expectations that we impose on ourselves or others. It can free you from the materialistic mentality we impose on ourselves every day. Whatever happened, happened. I would have to accept it for what it was regardless of the outcome.

When you feel like you're about to die, whether that's from running or some other barrier, put faith in the unattainable and trust your God given body. Stop giving a fuck and let go.

Also, how would you know if you're about to die? Have you died before? Do you know for a fact that if you kept going harder and further past your believed limits that you would actually die? Have you done that before in the past? If so, damn, you are hard!

Even when I get to the point of feeling like I'm about to die from going harder than I ever have before, I know I still have some gas in the tank. It's my mind that wants to quit. Not my body. I'll stare death in its eyes because I have already made a promise to God that when I die my body and soul will return to Him. Whatever I do that challenges me to a point to where I feel I can't go any further, I find comfort knowing that if I actually do die, that my body and soul will return to God as I have already bequeathed it back to Him.

See, I believe that what I have is not something that's mine. I didn't have it before this life so how can it be mine to keep once I die. It belongs to my creator. What I have is a gift that I get to enjoy for a short period of time, but once my life is over, my body and soul will return to its original owner. By accepting this as a truth, I don't mind living a life of suffering by being forged by the fire I get thrust into. I know I will become molded and changed forever after making it through the event. I will continue to exist in some form or fashion. This universe is all made of the same stardust.

I'm a stronger person now that I've analyzed most of the emotions I have been going through during my thirty plus inconceivable years. If you can get the time to go back and reflect about all the decisions you've made, during your whole life, and determine whether your emotions or your logical brain made that choice, I suggest you do that too.

Sometimes it takes an extreme life changing event for this to happen. Sometimes it may just be something you want to chase after. Regardless of what challenges you, make it a goal, figure out who you are and crush that goal. It's worth it. Not only will you find out who you are from an internal and external perspective, but you'll find out what you're capable of accomplishing.

Going through hardships makes you the person you are. Some are uncontrollable and some may be self-inflicted. Either way, you're meant to learn something from it. You should listen and quit putting blame on others. Look at yourself in the mirror and own up to you. It's you. It's always been you.

The key is, accepting what you've done and learning what you're meant to take away from it. If you never learn, you will certainly repeat it over and over again and never become wiser.

I am who I am. That has stood out to me forever. The gift that was given to us a long time ago was the ability to be forgiven and for us to forgive one another. To forgive each other and live with each other, with a type of unconditional love through forgiveness of each other's past, is the best thing we can do to save ourselves and the sanity of society. Be who you are, and I'll be who I am. Take nothing and leave nothing because you didn't bring anything with you in the first place. You are owed nothing. If you want to enjoy something in life you need to work for it. Earn it. No one will give it to you and don't expect them to either.

I know some have lived a worse life or had more difficult life events than myself. My heart goes out to them. I wish them the best and hope they can repent. They have the same abilities as all of us. The key is finding love inside of us and turning it on. Trust me. Once you ignite that fire inside of you, you will find a purpose. Just be sure to keep that fire lit and not let it smolder into hate.

I've spoken my peace. Everything else in life is yet to be lived. I have learned to run with all that life throws at me and to not run from it. I cannot keep quitting on myself. I will run through life with a humble stride and keep falling forward towards victory over the battles I have within. Through emotional awareness and intelligent insights, I have been forged into who I am. At the end of the day I have to accept that, I am who I am, because of who I've been.

From now on, I'll just run with it.

Recognition

To all that have forged me into "Who I Am"

Acknowledgments

Thank you for taking the time to read through my ramblings and perceptions. I want to acknowledge those that have helped me along the way and give them the opportunity to rejoice in my joy I have for them.

I'd also like to acknowledge myself and my own accomplishments for goals that I gave myself earlier in the book. If you don't recall, I set a couple of goals to get myself out of the hole I was in. One goal was to become a certified expert in a specific field of study and the other was to run a marathon.

I gave myself a year to accomplish both and I'm pleased to say that I completed them. Sort of…

I did sign up for a marathon and trained for months before it started but as usual, I fucked my legs up. I will note it wasn't the same injury as from my previous incidents. What had happened was, while on a long 10 plus mile run one day a couple months before the marathon was set to begin, I got a cramp in my upper calf. It sucked. It affected my training and it also affected my confidence in being able to complete a marathon.

So, I decreased my entry into the race from the marathon to a half marathon. I kept training as much as I could with the cramp in my leg and seemed to be healed up two weeks prior to the race. On race day I showed up ready to go. What I wasn't prepared for was the race's course. It was a 1 mile loop. I really should have done some research on the race I signed up for because I was not mentally ready for running around a loop for two hours. Either way, I did it. I completed the race in 100 degree Colorado sunshine in two hours and twenty two minutes. It was hot but I fell forward through it.

After completing the half marathon, I realized that I can compete and complete longer races. My next goal is to run a marathon but I'm not sure when that will be. Maybe I'll run a few more half marathons before going full marathon. Time will tell.

The other goal that I set out to accomplish was to become expert certified. Now, these tests usually cost up to five thousand dollars when you account for study material, travel, lodging and the cost of the exam itself. Luckily, I fell into an opportunity to take the exam with little to no cost. The only catch was that I only had three weeks to study. No way was I going to pass this test. Most people spend a year plus preparing for the exam.

I took the chance to sit the exam as a learning opportunity. No matter what happened, pass or fail, taking the exam would be a priceless experience I could use to take the exam again.

With that frame of mind, I studied my ass off for the next three weeks and mentally prepared myself for failing. When the day came to take the test, I was calm and prepared for the six hour exam. Yes, six hours. It's not an easy test and takes a ton of time to run through. After I finished the exam, I wasn't confident that I had passed. I was pretty sure I bombed it. I wouldn't find out for a few days if I had passed or failed and that really messed with me. I just wanted to know what the results were. Two weeks later I was given the results and I'm happy to say, I passed. I have no idea how I passed and was in disbelief for a while.

I ended up coming to terms that I passed the exam and now have a new goal to attack another exam. That exam gave me experience and the confidence that I needed to continue with that level of certification. I have now sharpened my sword and am ready for future battles.

Now for some recognition for those who are close to me and have had the most influence on me. I am grateful to have spent what time I've had with you all.

I want to first thank God's grace and His mercy He has had on me and the life He has allowed me to live. Without that, I would be nothing. I probably wouldn't even exist. All glory is His.

The most important person I want to thank is my Wife. I love you and want you to know that you have been my rock. You have always been there for me in my time of need and lifted me up when I was down. You mean more to me than you could possibly imagine. Thank you for your patience in letting me figure out who I am and always motivating me to keep falling forward. You are always there with encouragement and a perspective that I respect. Maybe a little negativity every now and then but that is also motivational. You know not to take me seriously and that I like to joke around and have fun. Though there are times when you understand that I'm not just joking around and that I might be crazy enough to be serious. #BradyBellForPresident2024.

I also wouldn't be alive if it were not for my Mother. You have always guided me towards safety through your love and compassion. I couldn't have expected to have a Mother as great as you. I can attribute all my strengths and stubbornness to you. You have shown me right from wrong and how to be a better man but especially, an outstanding parent.

As for my Son, thank you for coming into my life. You are truly a gift from God. You have shown me how to be patient, kind and loving in those times when it wasn't easy for me to be. I love you with all my heart and am blessed to have a son as special as you. You are so smart and so stubborn. Your Grandmother should be as proud as I am. You have qualities about you that cannot be replicated. God broke the mold when he created you.

Thank you for making me a father and showing me how to be unselfish.

My most precious Daughter, thank you for your loving spirit. You have given me a new heart. Your compassion and pure love have taught me to be a better human being. There is no other love that can compare to a father's love for his daughter. I will do anything to keep you safe and preserve your innocence from now and until the day I die. You have shown me how to be empathetic towards others and have given me hope for mankind. I pray that your light never fades.

For the two turds that beat my ass every day of my life as a child, I love you. I couldn't have expected anything less from the best two brothers on the planet. The day will come, when we are all old, and I'll finally have the upper hand to whoop your asses. You know how patient I can be. It's only a matter of time. Enjoy your youth, you old farts. But seriously, thank you for molding me into who I am. Without you I wouldn't be anywhere near who I am today. I am humbled to have two extraordinarily talented brothers who have taught me to stand up for myself and to not take shit from anyone. You two are the strongest human beings on Earth. In my eyes you are giants, mainly because you are so much taller than me, but you will never look as good as I do.

To all of my extended family I call friends and not acquaintances, thank you for coming into contact with my life and giving me a part of you so I can grow and learn from your life experiences. Without all of you I would be less of a person. I am grateful to have spent as much time as I have with every single one of you. Some noteworthy names for recognition; Karl, Josh, Eddie, Rob, Nick, Steven, Kenneth, Will, Matt, Marcus, Luke, John, Lewis, Omar, Britton, Sasa, Joe, Kevin, Chris, Jimmy, James, Andrew, Jason, and Brian. To all you other knuckleheads I didn't list, thank you as well. Just because your name isn't on the list doesn't mean you do not count. I know who you are, and you know who I am.

For the people who do not know me, nor do I formally know, I want to take a moment and recognize the impact you have made in my life.

To the unnamed musician, your words impacted me more than you'll ever know. You spoke the truth in the times when I needed it the most. Your life, as detailed through your music, resonated with who I was at the time and guided me to a better life. It got me out of the bad situations I was in but also gave me confidence to keep my chin up when all I wanted to do was to run away.

To the unnamed comedian, thank you for reminding me to laugh. Thank you for all of your hidden wisdom and fresh perspective. You helped me to forget about the mundane life and not be so uptight. You helped me to find my light in all the madness of this world through witty and snarky satire.

To the unnamed warrior, thank you for teachings and words of wisdom that inspired me to prove to myself that I had so much more potential in me. I would have never tapped into it if it were not for you. Thank you for teaching how to discover my mental barriers but also to keep falling forward and to never give in to defeat. I have pushed past limits that I thought were impossible. There is only one way out and that's by making it to the other side. I have a new perspective on what's possible, that is as long as I spend the time stretching before and afterwards.

To the unnamed world traveler and chef, thank you for showing me the people of the world and their culture. I wish you were alive so you could accept this gratitude I have for you. Your shows taught me that there is so much more to this world than my little plot. You showed us all to have compassion for our fellow man and that we all have one thing in common, the need to eat and cook food. So much could be resolved between our disagreements by starting with our common ground, like the need to eat.

To the unnamed public influencer, what can I say? You're the most honest and realistic person I have ever heard speak. Thank you for always being open to new concepts and spreading your insights to the world. You are an intriguing man whom I respect and have been able to relate to when it comes to dealing with all the different types of people in the world. It takes all kinds.

Lastly and most importantly, I want to thank YOU, the reader. Thank you for taking the time out of your life to read through my ramblings and getting to know who I am. I secretly wrote this book for you and not for myself. Well, maybe a little bit was for me. It's definitely something I can reflect back on when I start to drift away from what I preach. My whole goal is to share my thoughts and perspective in hopes that I could spread my knowledge to those who may need it the most.

For some of us, we just need to know that there is someone like us out there in the world. We need to feel accepted by our peers. We need to know we are not alone. I want you to know that there are people out there willing to truly listen to you. We want to hear your story. We want to get to know you. You are important. When you think no one else on Earth could possibly believe in you, I will. I am here for you because I care about you. We have more similarities than we have differences, and we need to start to live our lives in that manner. Let's put down our defensive shields long enough to know that our differences are really what we have in common.

We are all passionate about the same topics and need to find that common ground so we can be better than our past. Let's not look into the past so we can repeat it but rather learn from it so we can build a better future, together, as each other's servants. It all starts with a smile and a sense of inferiority. You can change the world with a smile and a simple authentic hello. I have faith in you.

If you want to change the world with me then start by changing your interactions with others. Give up your power trip for a general concern. We all want to feel important so let's start to show others how important they are to you. I can guarantee you will become important too.

Glory be to God and may Peace be with you, always.

Made in United States
North Haven, CT
07 May 2023

36361100R00200